Connecting Across Cultures

Global Education in Grades K–8

Connecting Across Cultures

Global Education in Grades K–8

Mary Ann Buchino and Bob Herring

ROWMAN & LITTLEFIELD EDUCATION

A division of

ROWMAN & LITTLEFIELD PUBLISHERS, INC.
Lanham • New York • Toronto • Plymouth, UK

ROWMAN & LITTLEFIELD PUBLISHERS, INC.

Published in the United States of America
by Rowman & Littlefield Publishers, Inc.
A wholly owned subsidiary of The Rowman & Littlefield Publishing Group, Inc.
4501 Forbes Boulevard, Suite 200, Lanham, Maryland 20706
www.rowmanlittlefield.com

Estover Road
Plymouth PL6 7PY
United Kingdom

Copyright © 2011 by Mary Ann Buchino and Bob Herring

All rights reserved. No part of this publication may be reproduced, stored
in a retrieval system, or transmitted in any form or by any means, electronic, mechanical,
photocopying, recording, or otherwise, without the prior permission
of the publisher.

British Library Cataloguing in Publication Information Available

Library of Congress Cataloging-in-Publication Data

Buchino, Mary Ann, 1953-
  Connecting across cultures : global education in grades K-8 / Mary Ann Buchino and Bob Herring.
    p. cm.
  ISBN 978-1-60709-990-1 (cloth) — ISBN 978-1-60709-991-8 (pbk.) — ISBN 978-1-60709-992-5 (electronic)
  1. Multicultural education—Study and teaching. 2. International education—Study and teaching. 3. Education, Primary. I. Herring, Bob, 1949- II. Title.
  LC1099.B78 2011
  370.117—dc22   2011005196

Dedication

To Sr. Carren Herring,
whose vision for student exchanges at Nativity School
started the course toward global education and to the
faculty, staff, students, parents, pastors, and parishioners
who continue to support our mission.

Acknowledgments

Global education at Nativity School began with the vision of Sr. Carren Herring and the support of Fr. Paul DeLuca. They believed that it was the right thing to do. We are grateful for this and their continued support as we have written this book. Our thanks to John J. Buchino, M.D. who told us from the start that we needed to write a book about global education at Nativity and, who has read and critiqued every version of our manuscripts. Our gratitude to Kent Peterson, Ph.D. who knowing about global education at Nativity School and having written some books himself, encouraged us to move forward on our own book and provided feedback on our efforts.

The faculty, staff, parents, students, and alumni of Nativity School offered their ideas and provided their insights during interviews. This book could not have been written without them. Our thanks also goes to the many teachers and principals of schools who also have a belief in global education and who shared their experiences with us as we researched current best practices.

The templates for the exchange of information about students and chaperons were graciously provided by Bev Campbell and Sue Bolduc of the International School-to-School Experience. We thank them for their generosity in allowing us to include these templates in our book.

Our manuscript has undergone several revisions with the audience in mind thanks to educational administrators, professors, and teachers who have read it and provided much needed feedback. We appreciate the time and comments from James Buchanan, Ph.D., Laura Herring, Joseph Maruca, Ed.D., Merry Merryfield, Ph.D., Paul Miller, Jim Rigg, Ph.D., Ryan Wertz, Ph.D., and John Waters.

Many thanks to Sue Ellen Brown, who volunteered to undertake what, to us, was a daunting task, organizing the index.

Finally, Tom Koerner, Ph.D., Vice President and Editorial Director at Rowman & Littlefield Education, was very patient with our never ending questions and provided gentle direction which has made this an incredible learning process.

Contents

Preface		xi
Introduction		1
Chapter 1	Global Education Across the Curriculum	5
Chapter 2	The Maps Program	25
Chapter 3	Student Exchanges	35
Chapter 4	Encouraging Teacher Support	61
Chapter 5	Encouraging Parent Support	71
Epilogue		77

Tables

1.1 Art from Different Continents	7
1.2 International Art Projects—A Developmental Approach	8
1.3 Music from Different Continents	10
1.4 International Music—A Developmental Approach	11
1.5 International Physical Education Activities	13
1.6 Rock Formations in Different Countries	19
1.7 Sample International Recipes	19
1.8 Sample International Foods	20
2.1 Changes to the Maps Test	28
2.2 Number of Items on Each Map Test	29
2.3 Possible Forms of Recognition for Achievement	32
3.1 Timeline for Student Exchanges—ISSE Model	45
3.2 Projects Week Committees	56
3.3 Friendship Project II	58

Appendix

i. Sample Map Test Study Guide	79
ii. List of Exchanges	81
iii. Sample Memorandum of Understanding	85
iv. International School-to-School Experience Forms	89

Preface

This Handbook for Global Education is intended to provide a framework for educators interested in opening the doors of understanding and appreciation for the global community. It draws upon the experience of Nativity School as well as schools that are members of International School-to-School Experience (ISSE).

Nativity, a K–8 urban Catholic parish school, serves an economically and ethnically diverse community in Cincinnati. Founded in 1921, it experienced significant growth with the post-World War II baby boomer generation. By the mid 1980s, the houses in which families with four, five, and six children grew up were now considered nice starter homes. Families who were looking for four bedrooms, a family room, and a two-car garage on a half-acre lot were headed toward the suburbs. The completion of I-71 put new subdivisions and the small towns in adjacent counties within a 30-minute commute to downtown. Enrollment was falling. Were Nativity's best years over?

In the summer of 1979 there was a change in administration both in the parish and in the school. The pastor, Fr. Stan Neihesal, soon to be joined by Fr. Paul DeLuca, and the principal Sr. Carren saw clearly the need for a more focused mission if Nativity parish and school were to survive. They got to work, consulting the community and adopting the best practices. The core of Nativity's mission was strengthened and new components were added: foreign language, computers, an emphasis on the arts, and the student exchange program. Nativity joined ISSE and in the spring of 1980 sent its first delegation abroad to Olinca School in Mexico City.

Imagine an ocean liner leaving Seattle headed due west across the Pacific Ocean. If it stays the course it will arrive on the Asian mainland north of Japan several weeks later. However, if the ship were to change direction by just a few degrees and head west/southwest, it would arrive in China or the Philippines after its voyage across the Pacific. The change of direction by just a few degrees can result in the arrival at a different destination. That's what the leadership team did for Nativity starting in the 1979–80 academic year.

The "back to basics" movement was strong in some communities in the early 1980s. Nativity had its share of those who believed that test scores would nosedive and student achievement would suffer if we made room in the schedule for artists in residence or visiting delegations from schools in other countries. The debate about the future of the school was intense; opinions were strongly held. Nevertheless, the leadership held firm and the commitment was made to the arts and the student exchange program.

When I was hired in 1984, the Interview Team was clear about many things. One of their priorities was global education. I discovered a community committed to a values-based education in an urban community that saw the opportunities that could unfold as the result of a strong commitment to the arts, technology, and global education. This had to be the best job in the whole world. And it has been.

Some people look at the world and see a scary place from which children need to be protected. The Nativity Community looks at the world and sees multiple opportunities for its students to learn, grow, and connect with others—opportunities to sharpen skills, enhance understandings, and form relationships. For this amazing community, the world is not full of threats and fear but is full of opportunities and possibilities.

Send a delegation to newly independent Ukraine, Kenya, or China? Of course. Host 84 students and teachers from China, Togo, Ukraine, Poland, Germany, and the Netherlands for a week all at the same time. Why not? Send students to an international summer camp in Europe? Let's do it! The student exchange program has been the most visible component of the global education program at Nativity and has received the most press. Equal to, and in some respects more important, have been the changes in the curriculum that touch the lives of all students every day through their nine years at Nativity. It took us awhile to understand that the best approach was not to add but to replace, for example, to make sure that the literature the students read reflects cultures from around the world rather than just our own.

Incredibly creative teachers have embraced the opportunity to integrate geography in math, science, literature, art, music, and physical education. Their story is told between the pages of this Handbook. The Nativity Community, urban and economically diverse, has supported the expansion of foreign languages (Latin, Spanish, and Chinese), and opened its doors to host students and teachers from around the world.

Throughout the economic downturns, the Gulf War, the aftermath of 9–11, the War on Terrorism, and changes in leadership within the parish, the global education program has continued to evolve and remain faithful to its mission. Therein lies the key to its success: Nativity is a mission-driven school. Agendas for the faculty meetings are organized around the mission of the school, and all decisions are made in light of that mission. In the very best way, the mission defines who we are and what we do.

In 1979–80 Nativity set sail into the future. The change in direction initiated then has resulted in a diverse urban school with a strong mission, a growing enrollment, and students prepared to be players rather than spectators in the global village of the 21st century.

Significantly limited by resources yet unlimited by imagination, over 30 years later Nativity continues to offer its students opportunities undreamed of when the idea first surfaced. It's the Friendship Journey, and it's time to change the world!

Introduction

> When I think of Americans now, I will no longer see guns pointing at us. I will see instead, the smiling faces of all the friends that we have made here. And, I hope, that when you think of Russia, you will see our faces and think of us as friends.
>
> —Juri Eliseev, Minister of Education for the City of Smolensk, Russia, 2006 International Projects Week

HOW DO YOU DEFINE GLOBAL EDUCATION?

Global education teaches students about the similarities and differences across people, their cultures, and traditions. It enables children to see the similarities—"a smile is the same in any language"—and respect and learn from the differences. As children learn about other nations and their citizens through every subject of the curriculum, they can begin to think critically about the factors that contribute to the differences among nations.

Is it the physical geography, the history, the population density, the weather, or the economy that causes people to live as they do, to have the traditions that they have? Recognizing how and why the people of other countries live as they do should cause students to question life in their own country. They begin to understand that "different" does not mean "wrong." It could mean a better way of doing things. At the very least, it just means different.

This type of learning takes place over years through meeting people from other countries, listening to speakers, knowing the location of countries, understanding the physical geography, and learning world languages. It happens because of discussions of current events and a global perspective incorporated in science and math. Appreciation of the contributions of different cultures comes through literature, art, and music. An understanding of play and competition is found in physical education. Children learn by watching the adults around them as they interact with people from other nations and talk about life in other countries.

The bottom line is a program that deepens students' understanding and creates positive attitudes toward other cultures. This Handbook provides a place to begin.

WHY CONSIDER GLOBAL EDUCATION AT THE ELEMENTARY AND MIDDLE SCHOOL NOW?

The Internet has transformed the world in the last 20 years into a smaller, more accessible community of nations. It has brought the global economy to cities and towns around the world connecting them in finance, manufacturing, and the selling of goods, services, and ideas.

The possibility that students entering kindergarten will work for a multinational corporation increases with each year. Many will accept assignments overseas or communicate with colleagues, suppliers, or manufacturers halfway around the world in the normal course of a business day.

The impact on universities is dramatic as course offerings expand and the number of college students spending a year abroad continues to climb at an ever-increasing rate. More students are learning Arabic, Chinese, and Hindi than every before. The number of passports issued each year continues to increase, as have opportunities in international travel for education, business, and leisure. In an effort to prepare students for a global perspective at the college level, state departments of education are calling for high schools and elementary schools to introduce global education into their curriculum.

WHY SHOULD GLOBAL EDUCATION BEGIN AT THE ELEMENTARY AND MIDDLE SCHOOL?

This Handbook for Global Education makes the case that elementary and middle schools are the places to start preparing students for their role in the global community. It is during these years that they are open to new ideas and new information. Through education they can increase their understanding and develop a respect for the cultures and traditions of other people. Opportunities that are present throughout the curriculum—from literature to science;

math to social studies; in art, music, and physical education—can provide the place to develop critical thinking as they compare and contrast what they learn with what they already know.

WHO COORDINATES GLOBAL EDUCATION IN A SCHOOL?

It is important for a school to have someone that oversees the global education program. The scope and sequence of information and experiences should have a definite direction and come together for students to help them understand how we are connected to the people of different nations. The global education coordinator can be an administrator, a teacher, or a staff member with an interest in the program.

Some schools have a committee with various components of the program divided among staff members. The primary components—curriculum, maps, student exchanges, and connection with parents and community—need someone who is committed to global education and understands the whole program. For a strong, comprehensive program to exist, there will need to be strong, coordinated leadership.

WHAT ARE THE COMPONENTS OF A GLOBAL EDUCATION?

Global education begins with the curriculum. The authors have drawn upon the experience of teachers and administrators who have intentionally integrated opportunities to link their students to the global community. You will find practical, proven suggestions for expanding students' understanding through all curriculum areas.

All the components of the global education program are linked by the maps. Creative teachers integrate geography throughout the curriculum and enable students to expand their understanding of political and physical geography. An earthquake in the Philippines, pirates off the coast of Somalia, the World Cup Tournament now have a place on the globe and can be seen in relationship to other nations.

In addition to the curriculum, attitudes change and understanding is enhanced when there is the opportunity for direct contact between students of different nations. There is a growing movement to bring a student exchange program to students in grades 5–8. Opportunities to exchange student delegations provide an experience unmatched by a DVD or classroom lecture. The authors identify the challenges and rewards of student exchanges along with practical suggestions of just such a program.

Everyone knows that change is difficult, especially for people who have a proven track record of success in any given area. Teachers and administrators already have a full plate and little, if any, time to add more to the "to do" list. This Handbook provides strategies to bring the staff on board in implementing a more inclusive, global approach to the curriculum.

As with any program, parent support is crucial if the program is to be a success. In the chapter on the role of parents, there are strategies that have worked in a number of schools. As children are exposed to new ideas and concepts, so too are the parents. They learn along with their children as they read the same literature, learn the location of new countries, or welcome students from abroad into their homes.

Consider this Handbook your passport to a new way of looking at education, a way that will prepare your students to be active members of the global economy and engaged citizens in the global village. It won't take place in one quarter, one semester, or one year. It's a journey that begins now. It's time to change the world.

Chapter 1

Global Education Across the Curriculum

Global education can be one big, open-ended adventure. The students learn about the people of other countries through the stories they read, games in physical education, art projects, music, and math. They learn from the students and guest speakers that they meet. When maps are used in all subjects, they're not just memorizing; the maps have meaning. They get a sense of "other." Children as young as kindergarten see the adults around them interested in the culture of other people. It becomes part of everyday life. It becomes part of who we are.

—Comment from a teacher in a school with global education across the curriculum.

Integrating global education into the curriculum is generally inexpensive and can add a special dimension to any subject area. It is best when done across all curriculum areas so that the students get a holistic picture of different cultures. They see cultures through literature, art, music, physical education, as well as math, science, and of course, history. In this chapter the reader will find suggestions for integrating global education into all areas of the curriculum.

LITERATURE

The list of children's books that focus on stories from other cultures is long indeed. Consultation with the school librarian or the children's librarian from the local public library is an excellent way to find books and stories that will be meaningful for your students.

In kindergarten as teachers introduce the alphabet, books such as *D is for Dragon Dance* provide a fun way to help students remember the sound that the letter D makes while providing information about Chinese culture. Additionally, folk tales such as *Stone Soup* from Sweden, *A Lion on the Path* from Africa, and *The Enormous Turnip* from Russia are great for quiet time and listening activities.

Primary-level language arts often teach students to explore word choices, examine different perspectives, compare and contrast settings and characters, and make inferences. Stories such as *Mulan* set in China can be read and then compared to the movie. *The Great Kapok Tree* tells the story of the rain forest in South America from the point of view of the animals. Books such as *Jalapeno Bagels* allow students to compare and contrast where they live and their favorite treat with the character of Mexican heritage.

Teachers in the higher grade levels may choose to use novels to read aloud to the class or to assign as class novels to be read independently or in groups by the students. Novels can be assigned at varying rates depending on the class, for example, one per month, per quarter, or per semester. Regardless of the rate of novels assigned, it is suggested that, whenever possible, a connection with other areas of the curriculum is helpful. The following novels are examples of those that relate to other curriculum areas.

- *Esperanza Rising by* Pam Munoz Ryan—After a sudden tragedy, Esperanza, a young girl living on a large plantation in Mexico with several workers and servants, finds herself fleeing to California with her mother to become a farm worker. The story unfolds during the Great Depression and presents a close look at Mexican culture and traditions.
- *The Egyptian Box* by Jane Louise Curry—When Tee's great-uncle dies, he leaves her an Egyptian shabti doll. A shabti, usually about 5"–8" tall, half-mummy, half-girl made of wood or stone, was placed in the tomb to accompany and serve the deceased in the afterlife. Tee's shabti comes to life and does the bidding of this sixth grader who doesn't like schoolwork or chores at home. This work of fiction fits well with the study of ancient Egypt.
- *Ties That Bind Ties That Break* by Lensey Namioka—This novel is the story of a young woman growing up in China in the 1911 when the binding of feet was tradition for all girls. Not having her feet bound is only the first tradition that Ailin Tao breaks away from in this story. Discussion and projects can focus on traditions in our culture as well as Chinese culture and how they have changed or remained the same over the years.
- *My Forbidden Face* by Latifa—This is an autobiographical account from the perspective of a teenage girl living in Kabul when the Taliban takes over. The impact on her family and friends and their eventual escape helps students to understand some of the issues related to the war in Afghanistan.

- *Night* by Elie Wiesel—The memoir of the author's time as a teenager in a Nazi death camp during World War II is both moving and graphic. This book is an excellent cross-curricular match with the study of World War II.

ART

As art teachers look at their overall scope and sequence, it is easy to find ways to fit in presentations about various artists and art forms from different countries. Art from around the world can be presented from a historical perspective, from a continent-to-continent approach, or from a developmental approach. For the teacher who wants to consider art from each continent, Table 1.1 offers some art forms that could be integrated into lessons during the year.

A suggested curriculum from a developmental approach would include some of the following ideas. In kindergarten through third grade students

Table 1.1   Art from Different Continents

Continent	Type of Art
Africa	Masks (wood, clay), sculpture (wood, stone), rock art, textiles (Fon Flag, Kente Cloth, Adire, Adinkra), body painting, basket weaving, bead work, headdresses
Antarctica	Sculpture (human,nin, animal, diamond), painting (landscape, abstract), ice art
Asia	Carving (gates, wabi style, silver), painting (Chinese brush, Vietnamese lacquer and acrylic, Japanese watercolor), sculpture (stone, wood block), ceramics (tea bowls, Neolithic vessels, textiles (silks, woven patterns), Mandalas, calligraphy
Australia	Rock art, bark painting, Papunya Tula (dot art), Aboriginal (leaf painting, wood carving, sand painting, weapons and tools), Atelier Method
Europe	Ancient Classical (murals, Greek & Roman sculpture, pottery), Byzantine (frescoes, mosaics), Medieval (iconic images, metal work, wood carving), Renaissance (realism, perspective, use of light/dark, contrast, texture and oils), Baroque (still life, landscapes)
North America	Folk Art (Canadian, Mexican), Native American (basket weaving, beadwork, pottery, masks, feather work, carved wood), Pop Art (advertising, comic books), African American (quilting, pottery, painting, woodcarving)
South America	Columbian art (pottery, gold work, stone, painting), Brazilian art (cave painting, Marajorore pottery, painting), Peruvian art (gold work, silver work, ceramics), Aztec influence

Table 1.2 International Art Projects—A Developmental Approach

Country	Activity	Level
France	Monet's Garden	Primary
France	Matisse—self portraits	Primary
Japan	Paper kimonos	Primary
Various African tribal groups	Clay masks	Primary
Ghana	Adinkra cloth prints	Primary
Mexican folk art	Tin suns	Primary
World cultures	Trip to Art Museum	Primary
China	Chinese Pottery at the museum	Intermediate
India	Mandala designs	Intermediate
Japan	Gyntaku prints	Intermediate
Austria	Klimt—pattern portraits	Intermediate
France	Gothic architecture	Intermediate
Germany	Medieval castles	Intermediate
Japan	Haiku tunnel books	Intermediate
Japan/China	Origami	Intermediate
Multiculturalism	Divinity chains	Intermediate
India, Malaysia	Batiks	Intermediate
Mexico	Diego Rivera—painted mural	Intermediate
China	Paper mache dragons	Junior High
Spain	Mina Creatures—crayon etchings	Junior High
Iran	Local art museum exhibit	Junior High
Spain, France	Picasso—cubist portraits	Junior High
France	Rodin—tape sculptures	Junior High
Spanish Moors	Escher tessellations	Junior High
England	Goldsworthy Matine Sculptures	Junior High
Spain	Dali—surrealist self portraits—	Junior High
Turkey	Islamic calligraphy	Junior High

learning about color, line, shape, pattern, and texture may enjoy the repeated pattern seen in an Adinkra cloth print from Ghana and other West African nations. These prints are done by carving a potato or carrot with a simple pattern then using paint to transfer the pattern onto cloth or paper. Clay masks with styles from a variety of African communities provide a hands-on demonstration of color, line, and texture.

Students in grades 4 through 6 can understand the concepts of balance and focal point. Presentations of Mandala designs of India, cathedral rose windows of France, and Celtic knots from Ireland fit with a historical perspective as well as an integration of previously learned concepts of color, line, and pattern. Malaysian dragons and Japanese origami help students to apply their own creativity to three-dimensional designs. Islamic calligraphy supports the study of Islamic nations, which is often done in the intermediate grades. This can be coupled with the study of the Islamic religion as one of many world religions. Field trips to cathedrals, mosques, and synagogues where cultural art can be experienced are also suggested.

Junior high students can work with the idea of real versus abstract in literature and in art. They also have a historical perspective through their study of American history. Discussion of the invention of the camera, Freud and the dream world, and World Wars I and II can enable students to see how contemporary artists viewed their world. Tessellation art and surrealist self-portraits can be done emulating the work of Escher from the Netherlands and Dali from Spain. A look at Picasso's cubist portraits and Matisse's self portrait offers the opportunity to compare and contrast works with a similar subject.

Collaboration with teachers of the core curriculum is another approach to integrating art from other cultures. Primary students may work on models of insects from around the world while intermediate students make an Egyptian sarcophagus along with their study of ancient Egypt. Junior high students might look at the influence of African art on the works of the Harlem Renaissance.

YouTube and pictures from the Internet provide easy access to everything from views of original works in museums, to how to do a project, to the final product. Table 1.2 is a sample of art activities done by one art teacher.

MUSIC

More publishers of music textbooks are moving toward incorporating music from other countries. Many textbooks come with CDs so that students can hear the songs and become familiar with the different rhythms.

As with the visual art program, music teachers may arrange their curriculum based on a historical approach, continent-to-continent perspective, using developmental issues, or they may want to integrate it with other curricular areas. Teachers can also choose to go by a certain genre, for example, marches, and explore it from the perspective of different cultures. They might include those of an American (Sousa) march, a Creole jazz march, and a march from an Italian opera. Another approach would be to "travel around the world" taking each continent and exploring the music of the countries on that continent. While the types of music and instruments of each continent are too numerous to list, Table 1.3 provides a small sample each.

In a developmental approach the kindergarten through third grade students would learn about pitch, rhythm, and pattern. The use of movement with song and call and response songs go along with the basic three pitches found in children's games from around the world.

Fourth through sixth graders can consider different styles and genres of music along with their historical references and the composers. Listening to the a capella style, students can discuss how it is used in ceremonial traditions from around the world and across the centuries. Taking a particular genre such as folk music, students can learn songs and compare beats from Europe, Asia, North America, and South America. As students become aware of the

Table 1.3 Music from Different Continents

Continent	Type of music	Sample Instruments
Africa	Singing as communication, West African highlife, Congolese Popular, Sabasaba, Kwella	Resonant solids (rattles, bells, stamping tubes, mbira), flutes (bamboo, reed, animal horn, gourd), musical bows (zither, lute, lyre), drums (goblet, kettle, cylindrical, barrel, hourglass)
Antarctica	Based on background of composers with use of sounds of nature (wind, water, whales)	Natural sources (ice, stone, water, feathers shells, bones)
Asia	Chinese ballads, opera, chanting, Japanese orchestral court music, Indian Hindustani, Carnatic	Chinese tamtam, Indian cymbals and bells, Japanese sakahachi, lutes, Jew's harp, mouth organ, Vietnamese board zither
Australia	Aboriginal music	Didgeridoo, bull roarer, clapsticks, Maori wind instruments
Europe	Opera, Classical, Chants, Celtic, Balkan, keening, wassailing, work songs	Bagpipes, mandolin, cowbell, concertina, castanets, accordion, alphorn
North America	Bluegrass, jazz, Native American (tribal flag songs and sacred songs), military music, big band	Native American (drum, horn, whistle, flute, rattle), Appalachian dulcimer, fiddle
South America	Latin jazz, Andean music, Cambia, Meringue, Reggae, Mariachi, Bolero, Candomba	Chilean guiterron, bandola, snare drum, marimba, bombardina, cuatro, Andean flute, maracas, tambora

Table 1.4 International Music—A Developmental Approach

Country	Activity
Canada, Greenland, Germany	Stories/songs with games—grades K–3
China	Traditional Chinese instruments—grades K–3
Japan	Japanese game/song—grade 2
China	Chinese National Anthem on recorder—grade 4
Cuba, North Africa, Brazil, Japan	Drumming techniques—grade 5
Mexico, Scotland, Israel, Austria	Dances—grades 6, 7, 8
Kenya, Hungary, Brazil, Mexico, Russia, Indonesia	Folk songs—grades 7 & 8

five-note scale and five pitch music they can learn to play the recorder and play songs from other countries.

Drumming is an area of music that most students enjoy. The rhythms and beats of drums from the Caribbean, East Asia, Brazil, North Africa, West Africa, Cuba, and Western Europe provide cultural lessons along with music. Teachers may find the music department of local colleges and universities, music stores, or stores such as 10,000 Villages willing to either loan the drums to school or come to school to do a "show and tell" for students.

Junior high students can learn the more complex rhythms. Vocal pieces that include three, and four, part harmony present multiple opportunities for the introduction to genres from around the world. This is also true for music instruction for students who play percussion instruments and recorders.

Students in all grades may enjoy learning songs in different languages. Again, teachers should look for textbooks and programs that provide CDs so that students can hear and see the pronunciation for the words in other languages. If world languages are being taught at the school, coordination with the instructor of each foreign language can provide support for learning songs.

PHYSICAL EDUCATION

Many physical education teachers look for ways to make the curriculum more interesting for students. Further, they want to find activities where all students can succeed. Using games from around the world can provide a positive response to both of these needs. For the kinesthetic learning, integrating multicultural games encourages an understanding and respect for different people from around the world.

Games can be coordinated with current events, cross-curricular activities with music, social studies, art, etc., in conjunction with the regular curriculum skills that enhance basketball or kickball skills, or a developmental approach.

In a developmental approach kindergartners through third graders would focus on gross motor movement and rhythm. So, for example, when teaching tinikiling (pole dancing from the Philippines), the poles would not move for the youngest students. Rather they would stay on the floor and the students would move their feet in and out with the one, two rhythm of the music. For second and third graders, the students would move the poles slowly. Faster music and pole movements can be used for fourth through eighth graders. Gross motor skills can also be enhanced through the following games:

- Norwegian Ball or Crossfire is played with four playground balls in the middle of the gym and two teams lined up on either side of the balls. For the younger students the team lines may be four feet from the balls. Older students can line up farther away. Students use volleyballs to move the balls across the other team's goal line.
- Indian Club Ball also teaches the skills of aiming with a ball, rolling and tossing, as well as catching a ball that is rolling. In this game, from 12 to 20 bowling pins, depending on the age of the students, are lined up across the middle of the gym. Half of the pins are blue and half are red. The object of the game is to roll or toss a ball and knock the pins down. The first team to get all of their pins down wins!
- Hungarian Team Handball helps students learn to dribble and throw a ball and is a good precursor for basketball and soccer. Suggested for students in grades 4 through 8, the students use a ball that is similar to a soccer ball that bounces. They dribble the ball, take three steps, and throw into a goal to earn points.
- Danish Rounders is a kickball game in which students run around the bases until the other team gets the ball to the pitcher. Students get points for every base that they run. Most students enjoy this high-scoring game because it does not demand a lot of skill. It can be used as an early step in the process of teaching baseball or kickball.

Folk dancing of various nations can also be taught as part of physical education. Dances from Israel, Mexico, Scotland, and Germany can be viewed on YouTube and taught in coordination with music class. For teachers who have students that do not enjoy folk dancing, it is suggested that the unit be alternated with a game from that country.

Table 1.5 International Physical Education Activities

Country	Game	Skill	Level
Ghana	Big Snake	Tag and group cooperation	Primary
Australia	Student in the Mud	Tag, running, crawling	Primary
Australia	What's the Time Mr. Wolf?	Counting, listening	Primary
Russia	Rabbits in the Wood	Chasing, running	Primary
Canada	Squirrels and Hawks	Tag, plan within a time frame	Primary, Intermediate
China	One, Two, Three, Dragon	In line group cooperation	Intermediate
Ethiopia	Spear the Disk	Aim, throwing	Intermediate
Israel	Hamesh Avanim (Five Stones)	Eye/hand coordination	Intermediate
Japan	The Lizard's Tail	Running, weaving	Intermediate
England	Fielding Race	Relay, bowling, running	Intermediate
Germany	Alpine Tag	Hunting, chasing, dodging	Intermediate
Mexico	Whirling Circles	Relay, whirling, rhythm	Intermediate
Argentina	Alto Ahi! (Stop There!)	Throwing	Intermediate
Australia	Wombat Ball	Hitting a ball, offense	Intermediate, Jr. High
Canada	Basketball Golf	Shooting a ball into a hoop	Intermediate, Jr. High
Brazil	1 Toque (One Touch)	Passing, kicking	Intermediate, Jr. High

Physical education teachers can assign a country to a group of students and have them research a game and teach it to the class. Information on the game should include: game title, country of origin, number of students on a team, supplies needed, grade level, and how to play.

MATH

Global information can be integrated into the math curriculum with some thought, time, and an Internet search for information. Population, distance between cities or countries, time zones, money exchanges, as well as the area of countries or deserts can readily be applied to math concepts at any grade level. Teachers may choose to focus on a particular continent or country, preferably one that coordinates with some other aspect of the curriculum. The following is a sample of the types of math problems that might be used in different grades.

- Kindergarten—When learning to count, worksheets can be made including pictures of animals, hats, musical instruments, or foods from around the world. These can be worked into word problems with simple addition and subtraction. For example, two kangaroos plus three kangaroos equal five kangaroos.
- First grade—Word problems may also provide information about special events in a culture. For example, every traditional Chinese household should have live blooming plants to symbolize new growth. Yushan's parents want to have blooming flowers in every room of their home and in every room of his grandmother's home. There are 6 rooms in Yushan's house and 10 rooms in his grandmother's house. They already have 8 plants. How many more do they need?
- Second grade—As students learn about temperature they can color in thermometers that tell the temperature in different cities around the world. The teacher can easily find these temperatures from the same day using the Internet. Showing the students where each city is located on a map completes the global awareness activity.
- Third grade—Adding and subtracting three columns of numbers lends itself to word problems that include a comparison of the length of rivers, the height of mountains and the number of stories in tall buildings from around the world. The Ohio River flows through Louisville, Kentucky, and is approximately 1,580 kilometers long. The Danube River flows near Tatabanya, Hungary, and is approximately 2,880 kilometers long. How much longer is the Danube River than the Ohio River?
- Fourth grade—More complex multiplication and division allows students to look more closely at daily activities of students in a particular country. If there are 2,000 students in Long Cheng Middle School and 55 students in each classroom, how many classrooms are in the school?
- Fifth grade—The concept of fractions becomes more interesting when students see relationships between continents. For example, the United States is 1/3 the size of Africa. If the area of the United States is approximately 9,158,960 sq. km., how big is Africa? There is daylight approximately 6 hours of the day during December in southern Finland. What fraction of the day do the Finns see daylight during December?
- Sixth grade—Data such as population of the capitals of various nations or the temperature in certain cities over a period of time can be used in graphing

and interpreting data. Students may want to work in groups to research, plot, and compare information from countries on each continent.
- Seventh grade—Junior high students can calculate the percentage of a population or the area of a city or country. The population of Togo is 6,458,605. If 35% of the citizens of Togo live in urban areas, find the number of people living in rural areas. Students might be given information from several cities or countries. Using that information they could calculate percentages and rank order the countries.
- Eighth grade—Changing dollars into euros, pesos, rubles, and other foreign currency requires computation with decimals. Students can convert American dollars into the currency of the nation and then research what they might be able to buy on their fantasy trip with a set amount of money.

I*EARN

The International Education and Resource Network (I*EARN) is the world's largest nonprofit global network that enables teachers and youth to use the Internet and other technologies to collaborate on projects that enhance learning and make a difference in the world. There is a US$280 fee for a school to belong or a US$40 fee for an individual teacher to join. I*EARN offers the opportunity for teachers in all subject areas to become involved in projects with teachers and students from many nations.

Projects can be a very simple one-session experience with students from one country to a project that involves several exchanges of information with students from several nations over the whole school year. Teachers enter the "teacher forum" online and look at projects by the age of the students or the subject area. When a teacher is interested in initiating a project, he/she contacts a facilitator to discuss the parameters of the project. If the specific focus, duration, and level of involvement have not been determined, then teachers collaborate online before bringing the students into the project. The following are examples of the range of projects.

Some activities use a blog format such as the *My Heroes* project where students write paragraphs about their heroes and then post them on the site. The teacher can go to the site and print sample paragraphs from students from different countries or show the paragraphs on an interactive white board. This project is available throughout the school year, so that teachers can use it whenever it fits into their curriculum.

- *The Christmas Card Exchange* has classes grouped with approximately six other schools and is done in November and December. Students can make cards, buy cards, tell about holiday traditions, and include pictures or any artifacts that they might choose to share the holiday experience with students from another country. Teachers then mail the packets of materials from their students to the students in all or some of the countries in the group. Students are usually thrilled to receive packets from the children in other countries.

- *Connecting Math to Our Lives* is a project that involves American students and students from one other country or a group of countries. The teachers meet online ahead of time and decide what the students will learn about each other and where they live—all done through math concepts. In the introductory email the students describe their class through the use of numbers. *We have 52 students in our class: 28 boys and 24 girls; 42 students are 9 years old; 10 students are 10 years old. Forty-six students live in houses and six students live in apartments.* The next exchange might deal with distance and information about the city where they live. *The fountain is in the center of downtown and it is 8 miles from our school. It is 43 feet tall. It was built in 1871. Our school was built in 1921. It has 20 classrooms. Most of the students in our class live less than 3 miles from school.* Students might also exchange information about their favorite foods, the types of pets they have, and their favorite activities so that the results could be used in graphing.

- *A Day in the Life* project works for most grade levels in that teachers collaborate ahead of time to determine a time line and topic or topics. Then students exchange emails or hard-copy letters telling about their routines on a typical day of school, summer vacation, holiday, weekend, field trip, or special event such as going to a wedding. This project also works well for students studying a foreign language.

SOCIAL STUDIES

Children in the primary grades like to learn about children from other lands in a very concrete way. Where they live, what they like to eat, and the games they play are just some of the topics that can be introduced using books and information from the Internet.

In grades 4 and above teachers can have students report on current events or sporting activities throughout the world. This information is easily accessible through the newspaper, magazines, or online. Web sites such as www.scholastic.com have information that is written with a vocabulary that most fourth graders can understand. A world map in a class where the countries that are being discussed and identified helps students to become familiar with their location and with their position in the world relative to the United States.

Special projects with guest speakers are particularly entertaining and memorable for students of all ages. They put a face, artifacts, and experiences together with the name and location of a country. This sort of activity can be arranged through the librarian, parents, or volunteers.

In one school the librarian decided to use the alphabet and have a speaker for a country that began with each letter of the alphabet. While it took two years to get through the alphabet, students in the primary grades listened to each presentation with interest and fascination. They can readily report what they learned about the countries.

Another model of using guest speakers uses parents, grandparents, friends, and fellow teachers who come into the class to talk about countries where they have lived or visited. Speakers bring artifacts and pictures. After the visit, the students write a journal entry indicating something they learned about the country. Songs about being friends with other children from other countries and children's songs from other countries are learned. At the end of the month-long experience, a potluck dinner is held with foods from various countries. The students come to the dinner wearing simple homemade costumes and perform the songs for their parents.

For schools that may not have family members or teachers who have traveled outside the country, teachers can contact the local college or university for speakers or use Google to locate the speaker's bureau for your city. Additionally, media, hospitals, and corporations often have employees who have traveled to other countries and will come to speak to school groups free of charge.

For older students a research project and presentation format can make learning about a different culture and peoples much more interesting than reading a textbook. In one such class, groups of students are assigned a country. They need to research the history, government, religion, traditions, arts, and foods. They also need to identify a person from that country that has made a positive contribution to the world. Students then meet with a native of that country and conduct a 45-minute interview.

At the end of the month-long assignment, each group gives a 15-minute presentation that includes what they learned about the history, government, religion, and traditions of the country. They also share something from the arts of the country. This might be some poems, songs, or a skit from a children's story. They provide a tri-sided poster displaying information about their country, as well as artifacts, a research paper, and food. After the presentations, which are viewed by parents and other students, the audience is invited to try the recipes.

For schools located in cities, immigrants or visitors from various nations can be located through universities, ethnic societies, and churches. The local mosque is likely to have citizens of Muslim nations who are very willing to help students learn about the Islamic religion and Muslim people. Likewise, the local synagogue usually has volunteers who will speak about Judaism and Israel. Understanding these cultures can be enhanced through a cross-curricular project with a visit to a synagogue or mosque through the school's art program.

SCIENCE

- Weather—Students can pick a city in another country and monitor the weather comparing it to the weather in their city. They can try to predict the weather patterns based on what they know of the location of the city relative to the equator and the location of their city relative to the equator.
- Natural disasters are often a high-interest topic for students in the intermediate and junior high grades. Learning about the Ring of Fire and the earthquakes, tornadoes, tsunamis, droughts, hurricanes, and floods along with the people of the regions makes the information more meaningful. Students may want to research how natives cope with these natural disasters in regions where they have a high frequency of recurring.
- Reptiles and Insects—Students in the primary grades are curious about reptiles and insects, and the stranger the better. Many books on these subjects show pictures of the reptile or insect and have a short summary about their habitat. Students can make a model of the reptile or insect along with a diorama of their habitat. Local zoos may have a program that brings insects or small reptiles out to schools so that children can see and touch them.
- Animals—Students can pick a continent or an animal and look at the causes related to endangered species. Presentations on endangered species easily become cross-curricular with art, language arts, or social studies. Students can make posters, start a fundraising campaign, or write a persuasive essay stating the reason that we should be concerned about a particular animal.
- Earth's Resources—Conservation of the earth's natural resources is a topic of global interest that can generate discussion, debate, and an action plan. Should forests be cut down to create much needed housing or farmland? How does industrial growth impact the water sources in different regions of the world? Where are the forests on each continent and how have they changed in the past century? Are minerals a renewable resource? What are kids in different countries doing to help conserve the earth's natural resources?
- Famous Scientists—Famous scientists are too numerous to mention in this text. They are, however, integral to a science curriculum throughout the grades. Regardless of the area of science being discussed, simply pointing

Table 1.6 Rock Formations in Different Countries

Rock Formation	Country
Karlu Karlu	Australia
Wave Rock	Australia
The Cheesewring	United Kingdom
The Externsteine	Germany
Perce Rock	Canada
Maltese Cross Rock	South Africa
James Bond Island	Thailand
Anah Rock	China
Goreme Valley Fairy Chimneys	Turkey

out on a map the scientists related to the topic and the country where he/she lived heightens students' awareness of contributions of people around the world. Older students can research famous scientists by gender, discovery, century, continent or area of science.

- Earth Science—Students often find the unusual occurrences in nature to be fascinating. Looking at pictures of rock formations located in various countries can bring about interesting discussions as well as memorable images. Seventy-five percent of the world's active and dormant volcanoes and 90% of the world's earthquakes take place in the Ring of Fire. Locating the "Ring" on a map and noting the countries and continents that are impacted provides a strong visual image for students.

- Health—Good nutrition is often a part of health lessons. Many grocery stores now carry foods from around the world. It is possible to create a few

Table 1.7 Sample International Recipes

Recipe	Country
Bavarian pretzel bites	Germany
Chocolate truffles	France
Biltong	South Africa
Apple cakes	Russia
Oven-fried cheese	Egypt
Fairy bread	Australia/New Zealand
Banana fritters	Madagascar
Hummus	Greece
French toast sticks	Canada

Table 1.8 Sample International Foods

Food	Country
mango	India
guava	Central America
kiwi	Italy, China, New Zealand
avocado	Mexico, South America
chickpeas	Middle east

lessons that introduce students to new foods along with information about other countries. Another approach to learning about countries and foods is to take one food, such as plantains, taste them and mark on a map all of the countries that grow plantains. Plantains are grown in several countries on six continents, for example, North America (United States), South America (Peru, Ecuador, Brazil), Europe (Italy, Greece), Africa (Cameroon, Egypt, Uganda), Asia (India, Malaysia, Taiwan), and Australia. Students can also tract the history of plantains, where they originated, and how they traveled to other countries.

TECHNOLOGY

Starting out with the basics of word processing, students in the primary grades can write short "reports" on a country using bold, italics, and underlining. Brochures about a city or country are good collaborative projects for pairs of students. This incorporates bullet points and can demonstrate the use of various fonts, sizes, and color with print. Importing pictures for the brochure is also suggested.

PowerPoint presentations have a great deal of appeal to students in the intermediate and junior high grades. They can learn about backgrounds and animation as they present information about the culture and traditions found in a country, a famous person from another country, or a historical perspective—"then and now"—for a foreign city or country.

Spreadsheets lend themselves to a comparison of cities or countries on as many factors as the teacher wishes to highlight. Population, average temperature, size of the city or country, height of the tallest building, length of the longest river, etc. Additionally, students can gather data points about population in the major cities of a country or the temperature of a city over a period of time and use the features of spreadsheets, such as finding the average or converting information into pie and bar graphs.

Skype is a free software application that supports video conferencing. Communication with over 25 countries is available with this program. It requires a computer with a webcam and microphone. Teachers can connect it to an interactive white board so that the screen is larger than that of a desktop computer. While it provides real time interaction with people in other countries its use is perhaps best when the audience (or class of students) watching and listening is limited to no more than three people.

Videoconferencing allows more than two or three people to interact through the use of software and the Internet. There can be either a dedicated system where all of the components are packaged into one piece of equipment or a desktop system, which requires adding on components to a regular PC. In either case the systems are generally not portable and should have a range of different cameras and microphones for adequate video and audio with a classroom of students. It should be said that users of videoconferencing report challenges with eye contact, the speakers can appear to be avoiding eye contact, and the delay in signal that can be distracting.

Telepresence is a sophisticated level of videoconferencing. It involves a software system that allows for real-time interaction with several people at either end of the conversation. It provides studio-quality video and audio such that those participating in the conversation truly feel as if they are in the same room. Both settings need to have the telepresense system. These products are very expensive, requiring an infrastructure within the computer systems that can support the audio and video demands. They do, however, provide an enhanced experience such that the students can interact with a large number of students in another country and feel as if they are sitting across the table from them. The audio and video with these systems is so clear that the audience can hear light laughter and see small gestures and facial features. Interactions where these products are used provide a feeling of intimacy and shared experience that is even more "real" than that experienced with Skype and other forms of videoconferencing.

WORLD LANGUAGES

The introduction of world languages can begin in any grade. The earlier, the better. Children at very young ages enjoy learning other languages and retain the skills longer if instruction continues over a period of years. One has only to turn on the television to see current children's programs with Spanish instruction or characters who speak Spanish. There are a variety of ways to introduce world languages into your curriculum.

Hiring a teacher, part time or full time, who can provide instruction in a world language is perhaps the best option that ensures a scope and sequence that fits your program and the needs of your student body. A teacher who is part of the staff provides the continuity from year to year and grade to grade. Additionally, he/she is able to collaborate more readily with other staff members so that information on culture, traditions, and language can be cross-curricular in nature.

When an additional staff position is not economically feasible, administrators need to be more creative. In one school collaboration with a local high school was arranged. The high school provided a teacher, who had a free bell at the end of the school day, to go over to a nearby elementary school to teach Spanish to the junior high students. A small fee paid by the students opting for Spanish provided a stipend for the teacher.

In another program a Memorandum of Understanding with a school in another country provided a teacher from that school to come to the school in the United States. The only costs were those associated with assisting the visiting teacher to obtain the appropriate visa. Families at the school provided room and board for the visiting teacher. The teacher, who teaches English in his/her country, had a year of English immersion and the experience of living in the United States. This gave the school of origin a teacher who was much better versed in English and in the customs and traditions of Americans.

There are a variety of software and online programs that teach world languages. While there is certainly an initial investment involved, the flexibility that they provide in scheduling and availability make them worth considering. Programs vary in the graphics, level of interactivity, and pace. Administrators and teachers are encouraged to try programs and speak to other educators that have used them before making a major investment.

If there are families in your school that speak a language other than English, you might consider asking for their assistance in your efforts to introduce other languages to the students. Parents might volunteer to do one or several lessons with a class. They might help in developing signs in their language that can be displayed around the school labeling the common objects, for example, door, flag, office, cafeteria, water fountain, library, etc. Some schools feature a display of artifacts from different countries, which might be borrowed from parents, in their main hallway each month. This colorful, visual teaching tool reminds students, faulty, and parents that this is a community that is interested in learning about others. One school that offers world language electives makes the standard introduction to the morning announcements (*Your attention, please. These are the morning announcements for Friday, December 15*) in a different language each day.

LESSONS LEARNED

- Global education can be introduced in all areas of the curriculum with little or no cost. It is limited only by the teacher's imagination.
- Use community resources whenever possible. Speakers, artifacts, and field trips make information about other countries more interesting to students and much more memorable.
- Start small by including global information in one subject per grade. As teachers in levels or departments share their ideas and experiences, the program will grow.

Chapter 2

The Maps Program

> Senior year of college I took an African Culture class. On the first day of class the professor handed out a map of Africa and told us to fill in the names of all of the countries. The implication was, "So you say you are interested in African Culture, let's see just how much you know about the basics. What are the countries in Africa?" After we finished he asked, "How many knew at least 5 countries? At least 10? At least 20? I remembered the location of about 25 countries. The only student who knew more than I did had lived in Africa when his parents were missionaries there! I felt surprised that I remembered so many countries and I felt pride in my elementary school for teaching us the map of the world.
>
> —From the memories of an alumna of a school with a strong maps program.

A map studies program is a key curricular component for global awareness. An article in Newsweek discussing geography as "The Forgotten Subject" includes a quote from a California 10th grader to his teacher, "I know this is a lot too late to be telling you. But I know nothing about maps. I mean absolutely nothing, not one thing. I don't know where the U.S. or L. A. or Calif. is located . . . I don't know the difference between countries, cities, town's [sic] or states. Can I have a little of your help please?" (*Newsweek*, September 1, 1986). Things haven't changed much in the last 20 plus years.

More recently, the National Geographic-Roper Public Affairs 2006 Geographic Literacy Study (accessed December 10, 2010, http://nationalgeographic.com/roper2006/findings.html) found that, although we had experienced three years of combat and approximately 2,400 deaths of U.S. military in Iraq, "nearly two-thirds of Americans aged 18–24 cannot find Iraq on a map" and "less than six months after Hurricane Katrina devastated New Orleans and the Gulf coast, 33 percent could not point out Louisiana on a U.S. Map" and "half or fewer of young men and women 18–24 can identify the states of New York or Ohio on a map of the United States. The study concludes that, "Taken together, these results suggest that young people in the United States . . . are unprepared for an increasingly global future."

The goal of a maps program is to help students become literate in physical and political geography appropriate to their grade level. There are, of course, several ways to introduce students to the continents, countries, and capitals of the world. Much depends on the level of detail, the amount of time to be spent during school hours, and the amount of time to be spent at home for students to learn the information.

Maps can be introduced to students at the preschool and kindergarten levels through puzzles and pages to color, cut, and paste. In some schools the introduction to maps begins in kindergarten, where students work with map puzzles and play map games that involve matching or colors. Primary-age students complete worksheets or do hands-on activities as enrichment or part of centers. Worksheets are generally organized by continent and involve wordfinds, ABC order, follow the directions coloring page, and pages on animals that are indigenous to the continent. Hands-on activities have directions for simple art pieces, for example, assembling three-dimensional birds, instruments, or toys. Each of these activities serves to help primary-age students in connecting countries with continents as well as basic information about the countries.

Map games for all ages are available at no cost on Internet sites such as www.maps.com and www.shepparsoftware.com/geography.htm. Teacher-made games that focus on continents and countries or countries and capitals can use a Jeopardy-type format on interactive white boards. Maps can be used on a daily basis in all subjects. The decision of what grade to begin a formal program with the study of the continents and oceans will depend on the type of students in your school and the amount of time in your school day.

More detail with respect to capitals, deserts, mountain ranges, rivers, bays, straits, and other physical features can be added to the study of maps as the students progress through the higher grades. A spiral curriculum whereby students learn more and more each year about the maps of North and South America, Europe, Asia, Africa, the United States, and Canada has proven to be a strategy that helps students to remember the information. The repetition involved, over five or six years, lends itself to the retention of the memorized material.

One model for assessing students' proficiency in the identification of countries, capitals, and important geographic features is to administer a school-wide map test once per month. Each month, the focus shifts from one continent to another. In September, students in grades 3–8 are given a continents and oceans test. October is North America, November's test is South America, etc. Map test dates should be on the school calendar and given to parents at the beginning of the year. It is suggested that the test date for each month be highlighted in a weekly school or classroom newsletter so that parents are aware of all test dates with plenty of time to help their child study for the test.

One school has found it helpful to have all of the students take the same test on the same day. They feel that this helps to minimize the potential for students to share answers with other students. It also helps parents and students to remember that "the test is coming up" because they will hear other students and parents talking about the test. The test may be given by the social studies teacher and, in order to be taken seriously, needs to count for a grade. In one case tests are turned in to the principal for scoring. Others may prefer to have the social studies teacher or the coordinator of the global education program grade the tests.

The theory behind the experience is that if students have a solid knowledge of the location of countries around the world, they also have a context for comparing governments in history, for looking at weather patterns in science, or population issues in social studies. The information they see and hear in the media has more meaning because they know where the countries are located. Knowledge of the location of countries, oceans, rivers, mountain ranges, and deserts provides context for a wide variety of disciplines but also for life.

HISTORY OF THE PROGRAM IN ONE SCHOOL

Most schools will find that like any addition to the curriculum, a map program will evolve depending on the time available and the learning style of your students. In a school that has students learning a large number of items on the world map, the program has evolved over the years. The culminating activity, after student knowledge of one continent per month is assessed, is to administer the World Map Test in May of each school year. This optional test asks students to, quite simply, identify the location of every country, major mountain range, major body of water, desert, and map demarcation.

In one school's example, there are more than 600 distinct locations to be identified. The student who receives the highest score receives the Amerigo Vespucci Award. The first student winner of the Amerigo Vespucci Award remembers, *I was in the first class to take the test. We were given blank maps of each continent and told to fill them in. I loved maps and used to spend library time looking at the atlas.*

During the early years of the maps program students were given a continent each month with just outlines of the countries, and they needed to fill in the names of each country. The number of items and the format has changed over the years. The test changed to a multiple choice format using Scantron forms in the early 1990s in order to save paper and ease the scoring process. As the map of the world has changed in the last 20 years, so has the test changed, for example, after the dissolution of the Soviet Union in 1989, the newly independent nations were added.

Other external assessments have also shaped the test. When a student missed a question about a desert during the 1999 National Geographic Regional Geography Bee, deserts were added to the map tests. In 2004, a dad with a bachelor's degree in geography won Principal for the Day at the

Table 2.1 Changes to the Maps Test

Continent	Items Changed to 4th Grade Test	New Items Added for 5th–8th Grade Test	New Items Added for 6th–8th Grade Test
Continents	Mediterranean Sea, Arctic Ocean, Arctic Circle, Antarctic Circle, International Date Line, Tropic of Capricorn	Bering Strait, Mediterranean Sea, Arctic Ocean, Arctic Circle, Antarctic Circle, International Date Line, Tropic of Capricorn	
North America	Greenland, Hudson Bay	Hudson Bay	
South America		Pampas (region), Patagonia (region)	
Canada	Arctic Circle, Hudson Bay	Arctic Circle, Hudson Bay	
Europe	Arctic Circle, Arctic Ocean, Ukraine, Mediterranean Sea	Turkey, Baltic Sea, English Channel, Vatican City	Balkan Peninsula, Jutland Peninsula, Iberian Peninsula, Italian Peninsula, Sicily, Scandinavian Peninsula, Prime Meridian
Asia	Arctic Circle, Himalayan Mountains, Ural Mountains	Sinai Peninsula, Dead Sea	
Africa	Sahara Desert, Tropic of Capricorn	Tropic of Capricorn, Atlas Mountains, Rift Valley	

Fall Festival Bid and Buy booth. One of his "duties" that day was to review the map tests and give his thoughts on what was lacking. He made several changes, lowering the grade level at which some items were introduced and adding other items.

Introducing the Maps Test

For one school the maps program in its current state is a spiral curriculum that begins in third grade. Third graders take the continents test, along with the fourth through eighth graders, in September. Fourth through eighth graders take additional tests, one each month. The tests are developed, distributed, and scored through the school office, which encourages the teachers to support the program because it is not adding to their already full load of classroom duties. An additional benefit is that this allows the principal or program administrator to monitor student progress, make changes in the test as needed, and gather data regarding student achievement.

The administrator of the program may also want to make a mental note of student grades on tests so that he/she can talk to students directly about their scores. This connection with the students from an administrator reinforces the message that "This program is a priority in our curriculum." The chart below outlines the time line and content of each test.

For schools with students who are used to taking tests on the computer, the multiple-choice format of the map tests easily lends itself to software

Table 2.2 Number of Items on Each Map Test

Month	Content	# of Items 3rd Grade	# of Items 4th Grade	# of Items 5th Grade	# of Items 6–8th Grades
September	Continents and Oceans	13	25	40	40
October	North America and Island Nations		28	43	87
November	South America		25	34	49
December	Canada		18	28	28
January	Europe		15	50	114
February	Asia		13	93	114
March	Africa		15	75	87
April	United States		118	126	146
May	Optional World Test				642

programs such as Exam View. This software package allows the students to take multiple-choice tests with immediate scoring afterward. It will also randomize the items so that students sitting next to each other will not have the items in the same order.

In this school third and fourth graders are taught the map information in class. Students in fourth grade use Mapmaker software to color, mark, and highlight the countries and map demarcations that they need to know for each month. While time is spent in class with each student making his/her own map, the students, ultimately, need to spend time at home reviewing the countries, oceans, and map demarcations. In fifth grade the teacher goes over the map information two or three times during the month. An interactive white board is used for interactive activities that help students focus on the items that they need to know. The expectation, however, is that students will practice and memorize the information at home.

The Map Test for Grades Six Through Eight

The maps contain the full compliment of items each month for the sixth, seventh, and eighth graders. Sixth graders are given the study guides with the outlined maps similar to the previous years (Appendix i). During class time the teacher presents a variety of strategies that can be used for independent study of the maps. Since most of the test is a repeat of what students have done for the past three years, seventh and eighth graders are given the study guide and a blank map at the beginning of each month and are required to review the information on their own time.

In a school where students do not have ready access to the Internet at home and there is less parent involvement, the junior high social studies teacher presents only the countries through work sheets and games during class time twice per week. Map activities use only a small part of the whole class instruction and are also left for when students finish their work or have time during the library bell.

National Geographic has recently introduced the Giant Maps Program (events/nationalgeographic.com). Schools can rent a map of Africa, Asia, or North America (more continents will be coming) for two weeks for $450 with additional weeks costing $225. The maps are approximately 26' by 35' and weigh approximately 145 pounds, requiring a gym or other indoor space for display. They are made of sturdy vinyl such that the students can walk on them without shoes. Each map depicts the countries, capitals, mountains, and deserts. The maps come with a trunk of activities and materials that allow students to experience the map through games and body movement. The activities are appropriate for kindergarten through eighth grade and are a great teaching tool for the student who uses visual and/or kinesthetic means as his/her primary learning style.

While a spiral curriculum approach to learning the maps has many advantages, it can present a problem for students new to the school, especially when entering in junior high. Therefore, when new junior high students enter the school, school personnel must take time to familiarize the students and the parents with the map program. Parents should be given the study guides as soon as possible before the student enters so that he/she can study over the summer or early in the school year.

A caution should be given that new students will hear their peers saying that they don't need to study that much for the tests. And this may be true for many students. A review a few nights before is enough because they have had these tests for the past four or five years. New students need to understand that. It is not that the test is easy. It is that the other students have studied the information so many times in the past that they do not need to spend a lot of time at this point.

THE WORLD MAP TEST

Research shows that high academic expectations lead to greater student achievement. In short, what schools ask students to do plays a large role in what they will be able to do. A world test is a strong example of an incredibly high expectation. In order to elevate the status of learning the items on the map tests, a World Map Test that demonstrates a level of mastery can be an optional test that is open to the students in the higher grade levels in the school.

While few students may participate in the initial years of the program with time and the right combination of highlighting of participants, the program should grow to at least 30%–40% of the students participating in this activity. Because of the comprehensive nature of the test, it is suggested that the test be given after school in May. The number of items and format of the test may vary depending on the school goals regarding the map tests. The World Map Test may have as few as 245 (195 countries plus the 50 United States) or as many as 642 (includes some capitals, mountain ranges, deserts, oceans, bays, peninsulas, and global demarcations).

A generous but defined period of time should allow students to go at their own pace. The test should be prepared, proctored, and scored by the global education coordinator. A fill-in-the-blank format where the student needs to identify indicated items or, like the monthly tests, in a Scantron format would be the two best options for the test.

Table 2.3 Possible Forms of Recognition for Achievement

Scores	Certificates	Trophies	Medals	Flags
Below 70%	Certificate of Participation			
80%–90%	Certificate of Achievement	Small Silver Globe		One flag
7th–10th place	Certificate of Achievement	Small Gold Globe		Two flags
4th–6th place	Certificate of Excellence	Large Bronze Globe	Bronze Medal	Three flags
2nd & 3rd place	Certificate of Excellence	Large Silver Globe	Silver Medal	Four flags
1st place	Certificate of Excellence	Large Gold Globe	Gold Medal	Six flags

All students who take the end-of-year World Map Test should be recognized publicly in the manner that other award winners are recognized, preferably at an honors assembly at the end of the school year. This adds "value" to the effort needed to take the test and the status of the test in the view of the school administration.

Traditional awards such as those given for sporting events can be adapted for recognition of the participants and winners of the World Map Test. Schools may choose to keep the awards in the same genre as are given for other events. The idea of giving small flags in a stand provides a more "global" touch to the award. Flags may reflect countries that have had student exchanges with the school or a flag representing a country from each continent. Each school will have a different meaning for the flags that they choose to use in the awards ceremony.

The highest scorer should also have his/her name on a plaque in the Hall of Honor, Awards Display Case, or public area of the school commensurate with the highest award winners of other school activities. Depending on the location of the school, the global education coordinator may want to consider the possibility of finding a sponsor, that is, a business that has international connections, that would want to offer a small monetary award for the student with the highest score.

As the school culture grows to embrace global education, the status of the award will grow. At one school the Map Recognition Award is the last award given during the honors assembly and the applause from the student body rivals that found at sporting events. The culture has evolved in such a way as to value global education and this award so that "it's cool" to be the winner.

Schools may find that they have few repeat winners. One "Triple Crown" winner with the highest scorer on Word Map Test in 1988, 1989, and 1990 had near perfect scores each time. Now a social worker in Japan, he remembers, *It was easy for me. I really didn't have to study much. I just always loved maps so the monthly map tests and the World Map Test were fun. It was amazing at the Awards Assembly to have the whole student body clapping for me. It's the only standing ovation I've ever gotten!*

Accommodations

Many students with special needs have excellent visual memory skills and score high consistently on map tests. This appears to be due to the multiple-choice format and the fact that the student really needs to only recognize the name of the item or sometimes just the first letter of the item. The test also lends itself very well to mnemonics for the auditory learner and to a kinesthetic approach, cutting out the countries and arranging on the continent outline like a jigsaw puzzle.

The map tests, particularly Europe, Asia, and Africa, can be daunting for students who struggle with memory activities. One accommodation that can be helpful is to continue to use the fourth grade map test for students in higher grades. The test basically looks the same as the others, just somewhat shorter. Of course another easy accommodation would be to limit the number of choices to two or three rather than four.

CONNECTING MAPS TO THE CURRICULUM

While the names of countries, capitals, and geographic features can be memorized like any other information in any other subject, it is much more likely to be retained if the facts being memorized are related to a bigger issue. For a school that has global education as its mission, providing exchanges with students from around the world and integrating global information throughout the curriculum, the use of maps in every subject is a natural context for supporting the names and locations of countries, capitals, and geographic features. When a school does not have such a highly integrated program of global studies, the administration and faculty should consider how they will make maps meaningful to the student. What topic can be used to tie together map studies throughout the grades? Is there a topic that is more appropriate for particular grade levels? For example, the topic of "endangered animals" could be used in the primary grades, while "extreme weather" might be more interesting to students in the intermediate grades.

Another approach to making maps more meaningful is to highlight the connection between the products that we use and their origin. Again, this sort of activity could be done each year choosing a product of interest that is appropriate for the age level. Younger children might be interested in where chocolate comes from, while older students might be interested in how we get gas for cars.

LESSONS LEARNED

- Since knowledge of the contents of the maps tests is not one of the state standards for any grade, the program needs strong administrative support in order for teachers to follow through with preparing for and administering the tests.
- It is important to have parents "on board" with the program. They need to understand why the teachers and administration are asking students to learn world geography. One of the best ways to explain this is by using current events, for example, pirates off the cost of Somalia. Where is Somalia?
- While they are in the elementary grades most students do not appreciate the value of memorizing the location of countries and major geographic features on a world map. Many, however, will tell stories of how surprised they were to find out that their peers in high school, college, and graduate school did not know the location of countries where major world events were taking place.
- Students remember the names of countries, capitals, and geographic features because of the spiral, repeated approach of the program but also because the information is related to what they are learning across the curriculum. It is important that the memorization of information from maps is connected to the people, products, or events of other countries.

Chapter 3

Student Exchanges

I was on the first exchange to Kokkola, Finland. It was pretty different. We went in February so it was really cold. There was about two feet of snow covering the whole town. The kids never miss a day of school. They (cross country) ski to school. I remember that it got dark fast. On the weekends they did stuff like go ice fishing. They drove the car right onto the ice! They would sit in a sauna then walk out in the snow and swim in the lake! In school the kids didn't wear shoes and they all knew more than one language. One night for dinner we had meat and the family told me it was beef. After I tried it they told me it was reindeer! I brought Skyline Chili and we made if for dinner one night. They loved it! Elina and I have stayed friends all these years. She came to Cincinnati a second time, we met in England a few years ago and we send emails. I learned that everybody has a different story, and regardless of the language we speak, we are all alike. The Finnish family had dinner together, the kids did homework and played games. I think it's good for students to be a part of an exchange in the elementary grades because you are open to learning about a different culture.

—Comments from a student on an exchange with Finland

Student exchanges can be at the heart of a global education program. For students who travel to another country or host visiting students, the experience provides interactions that become friendships, some of which last for decades. For all students, meeting children from other countries provides an awareness of other cultures that is attached to faces and names. Knowing people from another country makes information in books and events presented in the media more meaningful as the country is no longer a vague, far-away place. It is people that you know and remember. The country now has a face and the people of the country have a name.

A good place to begin exchanges is through the International School-to-School-Experience (ISSE) Program. ISSE is a non-profit, non-political, and non-religious program that arranges a partnership between schools from different countries. The exchanges are aimed at 10 to 12-year olds with the belief that a student of that age is mature enough to benefit from the experience yet young enough to be open to people of other cultures and free from prejudice. There is a fee for a school to join ISSE and a meeting every other year for the random pairing of schools. Countries currently included in ISSE are Australia, India, Costa Rica, Mexico, Ecuador, El Salvador, Japan, the United State, Malaysia, Peru, and China.

In the initial stages of proposing a student exchange to parents and teachers there may be some resistance. Sending sixth graders far from home, having them miss instructional time, and going abroad can be significant concerns. Generally, once parents see what their children gain from the experience of living with a family in another country, the word spreads regarding the value of an exchange program. (See Appendix ii.)

Administrators and staff need to be on the constant lookout for potential exchange experiences. The Sister Cities Program can be a valuable resource for an initial step in finding schools that would be interested in exchanges. Located across the United State, the Sister Cities International is an American, nonprofit, citizen diplomacy network that creates and strengthens partnerships between U.S. and international communities. There are more than 2,500 communities partnered with 126 countries.

One example of the potential available through the Sister Cities Program happened when a Ukrainian teacher, visiting Cincinnati through the Cincinnati-Kharkiv Sister Cities Project, was interested in seeing schools and sharing information about newly independent Ukraine. A Cincinnati principal invited him to meet with his students. Discussions led to the idea of an exchange between the school in Ukraine and the American school that he visited. Using the Cincinnati-Kharkiv Sister Cities Project as a resource, the principal followed their procedure for developing a Memorandum of Understanding that outlines the time and responsibilities involved in student exchanges. In 1993 the American school in Cincinnati and the Ukrainian school in Kharkiv began a relationship that has continued to this day.

Another example of a connection made through the Sister Cities Program is a partnership between a school in Liuzhou and a school also in Cincinnati. Prior to the two schools meeting, the Cincinnati-Liuzhou Sister Cities Committee had established a program for teachers from China to visit Cincinnati for three months each year to learn about education in the United States. An American school interested in a connection to China approached the Cincinnati-Liuzhou Sister Cities Committee to explore the options.

With the endorsement of the Cincinnati-Liuzhou Sister Cities Project, the government of Liuzhou was open to considering the partnership. Contact between the two schools was established and the conversation began regarding program goals, funding, and timeline. Several months later both schools agreed on a Memorandum of Understanding that would govern their relationship for five years. The Memorandum called for the following:

- An exchange of student delegations in even number years starting in 2008.
- Professional development opportunities provided by the American school for the instructional staff of the Chinese school in the area of teaching English as a foreign language.
- Instruction in Chinese language, traditions, and customs for the American students. Each year a teacher from Liuzhou would teach Chinese to students in grades 4–8 in exchange for housing, meals, and access to cultural opportunities in Cincinnati. This provides an English language immersion experience for their teachers of English and a teacher of Chinese for the American students at no significant cost to the school.

Depending on the country and cultural protocol, Memoranda of Understanding (Appendix iii) may be done totally through email or in person. It is best to consult with the local Sister Cities Committee to determine the best way to proceed.

A partnership with Torkinmaki School in Finland began when a Finnish professor of economics posted a request on an electronic educational bulletin board in January 1995. He was looking for an economics professor in an English-speaking country interested in a partnership where his students could collaborate on a project with native English speakers that would enhance the students' understanding of business concepts and correct use of business vocabulary. An American principal responded to his posting, noting that his school was an elementary school and not what this professor needed, but asked if he knew of any elementary schools in Finland that might be interested in working with a school in America. The professor responded, "That would be my brother, the principal of Torkinmaki School."

Since the American principal was going to be in Paris with an exchange through Association for French-American Classes in March and the Finnish principal was going to be in Brussels at a meeting of European Union educators, they agreed to meet in Brussels. At the Hotel Metropol Cafe they worked out the first draft of a Memorandum of Understanding on a napkin calling for a student exchange to take place during the 1995–96 school year. This memorandum (see Appendix iii), which has been renewed every five years, provided for the following:

- An exchange of student delegations
- A teacher exchange
- An exchange of student art.

Dr. Peter Johnson, now Director of Education in Kokkola, Finland remembers:

The face-to-face meeting in Brussels was important, because in the first place, in 1995 our teaching staff at Torkinmaki School was not willing to start the co-operation with a school from America, because they thought it would be impossible. In retrospect it seems that if we have a detailed plan and lots of good will, most of our dreams will become true. After these 15 years of co-operation the teachers as well as the parents and the students are very happy that Torkinmaki School made a new and positive decision in autumn 1995.

Talking to directors of global programs that already exist within the city or region can lead to connections with schools in a variety of international locations. These programs may be created through the local university, through contacts with international corporations, or through contacting the local church, mosque, or synagogue. Suffice it to say, the potential for connecting with the leadership of schools in other countries is limited only by one's imagination, time, energy, and interest!

ARRANGING THE EXCHANGE

Once the connection is made with a school that wants to do an exchange, the principal or coordinator of the exchange program will want to exchange emails with the principal of the other school. The contents of the correspondence are possible dates for the visits and the size of the group that can travel. The size of the group is a function of the number of host families available and the comfort level of the chaperones. When that information is established, a letter goes home to the students in the appropriate grades stating the dates of the exchanges, the names of the chaperones, and the approximate cost.

It is recommended that the cost should be limited to the following:

- Round trip airfare
- Passport fee
- A gift for the host family
- A reasonable amount for souvenirs
- Any participation fees for the exchanges.

An additional cost is the airfare for the chaperones. One school divides their airfare by the number of students going on the trip and adds that to each student's fee. Other schools cover the cost of the chaperone's airfare through funding by the PTO or through their professional development fund. The local community will know best how to cover those costs. A contact person should be identified so that parents can call or email with questions. A non-refundable deposit for those intending to participate should be due within 30 days so that there is a definite commitment on the part of the parents. This allows the exchange coordinator to move forward in planning for the number of host families needed.

STUDENT SELECTION

At one school all students who want to go are accepted. The only limitation is the number of spots available from host families. If there are more students than spots available, then students complete an application stating why they want to go, what they think they will learn, what concerns they have about going, and a question or two that provides an idea of how they might represent the United States (e.g., describe the American dream.) Other considerations in the selection include the opportunities for the student to go on another exchange or whether he/she has already been on an exchange.

Some schools use the exchanges as a reward or motivator for good grades, the philosophy being that the students will miss class and need to make up work. Generally, it is students with strong academics that can handle missing two to three weeks of class. Other schools make an application and interview a routine part of the process of selecting students for an exchange. They want the best representatives of their school and look for a maturity level regarding the ability to be away from home.

Schools that have instruction in world language or world language clubs often give priority to the students who know the language of the country that they are visiting. Some schools try to include an introduction to the language of the country to students who will be on the exchange. The instruction usually presents simple words or phrases.

CHAPERONE SELECTION

Chaperone selection can be done in a variety of ways. In one school there is a Chaperone Selection Committee that is made up of the principal and faculty or staff members who have been a chaperone. Decisions about chaperones can be made within one meeting regardless of the number of committee members in attendance.

Decisions to be considered when deciding eligibility include:

- Are all full-time (maintenance, instructional assistants, administrative assistant, etc.) employees eligible or just faculty?
- Can part-time instructional and support staff be considered?
- Is there a minimum number of years on faculty before one can be considered?
- Is priority given to staff with more seniority?
- Is priority given to staff that have not yet been on an exchange?

In other schools the administration and the coordinator of student exchanges conduct an application and interview process similar to that used to select students. Consideration is given to length of time teaching at the school, ability to speak the language of the country to be visited, ability to connect with students, organizational skills with students, and overall flexibility.

Whenever possible, there should be two chaperones and at least one should be experienced in the process or, at least, in foreign travel. This is particularly helpful in the event of the hospitalization of a student or other unforeseen situations. Additionally, an effort should be made to have a male and a female chaperone. Consideration might also be given to the interest that the staff member has shown in global education and/or delegations that have come to visit the school.

It is highly recommended that the principal or coordinator of the exchanges go as a chaperone on all inaugural exchanges. This helps to solidify the connection between the schools since that person has done all of the communication up to this point. It also enhances the trust of the families of the students who are going on the exchange and that of the hosting families.

COMMUNICATION WITH PARENTS OF BEFORE THE EXCHANGE

Approximately 10 days before departure there should be an informational meeting for the parents. It is suggested that the principal, the exchange coordinator, and the chaperones are present to discuss the following agenda:

- Introduction of all parents and students.
- Information about the partner school.
- What to wear—uniform (if there is one), travel outfit, one good outfit for meeting with government and educational officials.
- Money—suggested amount for spending and how to convert money.
- Communication system—email/phone chain for disseminating basic travel information and updates to the families.
- Logistics of meeting at the airport—what time and where to meet.
- Bag tags—clear identification on the outside and the inside of the suitcase.
- Procedure for unexpected occurrences—including terrorist attacks or suspended international travel.

A major point of discussion at this meeting is the fact that ***THIS IS NOT A VACATION***. It is work. The students are representing their country and most often are the first Americans that the host students and families will meet. Up until now their knowledge of Americans has come from TV, movies, newspapers, and the Internet. The U.S. students need to hear very clearly, *They will get their impression of Americans from you. Everyone will be watching you in the homes, at school, when you are in the community. You will answer the same question dozens of times per day. You need to not be tired, cranky, and impatient. You need to be gracious and have a smile. We will help you to state your needs, for example, time to rest, but you need to understand that you will be "on" the whole time that you are in the hosting country.*

MISSED SCHOOL WORK

It is best to plan exchanges so that they overlap with a school vacation. This reduces the amount of instruction the students will miss. This being said, most exchanges are two to three weeks long so that at least one week of classes is missed. Because student exchanges are considered a school-sanctioned learning experience, the expectation is that teachers will accommodate the students wherever possible. It should also be understood by students and parents that students are accountable for work, tests, quizzes, and projects that are missed. Teachers need to work with students to ensure that, as much as possible, schoolwork is covered either before or after the trip.

In subjects like math, science, and social studies students can be given work so that they can "work ahead" or catch up when they return. Some assignments might be modified and dates and times for tests can be changed to accommodate the amount of time away as well as a few days back to recover from jet lag. In language arts a writing assignment based on the experience of the exchange can often takes the place of other creative writing assignments that were done by students who did not go on the exchange.

It is suggested that there is a firm guideline for the date that all work is due when the students return from their exchange experience. That way both students and parents know up front the expectations regarding schoolwork.

COMMUNICATION WITH HOST FAMILY BEFORE TRAVELING

Once the roster of students going on the exchange is established the list should be sent to the host school. Matches are made and email addresses are exchanged. Both parents and students use email to get to know each other in the time before the trip. Information such as allergies and general likes and dislikes are discussed so that the host family can be as prepared as possible for the visiting student. ISSE has developed forms for this purpose (Appendix iv).

Suggested Chaperon Responsibilities

- Building "Team USA"
- Team meetings
- Passports & tickets
- Daily check-in with students
- Communication with parents and school officials—daily (or as often as possible) emails
- Liaison between host school and students
- Hosting visiting chaperones
- Culture show preparation
- Class presentations at host school

TEAM USA

Chaperones should begin meeting with the delegation approximately two months before departure. In one school they meet approximately six times for two hours per meeting. The purpose of the meeting is first and foremost to build a sense of "Team USA." Since the delegation may be a mix of students from different grades, they need to shed their identity as "sixth graders" or "seventh graders" and become part of the school delegation representing the United States. Initial meetings can be spent in team-building activities and having the students share what they have learned from their research about the country.

TEAM MEETINGS

The second goal of the meetings is to plan a cultural show, the class visits, a display, and any other group presentation that students might want to do. A cultural show that can be done in a 30-minute presentation in front of the whole host school is often appreciated by the host school. Since most students from other countries have some familiarity with the big cities of the United States, the goal of this presentation is to help the students of the host school to learn about your city or town. A typical format involves a narrated PowerPoint with information about school of the visiting students and their city or town followed by an American folk song and/or dance. The show needs to be planned by the students and practiced so that they are comfortable presenting with a microphone.

Many host schools enjoy having a display in a main hallway or meeting area that provides a visual introduction of the visiting students. The students might bring pictures of themselves with a brief note about themselves, pictures of their school, town, or city, and a map showing where their home is located. The materials for this display should be planned and organized by the students.

Classroom visits need to have an activity and content that is age appropriate. So, if they will be visiting with younger children, they may decide to teach them a game or a nursery rhyme or song. For older students they may want to explain American football or baseball and bring postcards or pictures that show local sports teams.

Chaperones also need to talk to the students about how to interact with people that they have never met. Suggestions for conversations starters are much appreciated. Students should become familiar with the host nation's culture and they should practice the appropriate way to greet people, show gratitude, and bid farewell that respect the local customs and traditions.

IMPACT OF STUDENT EXCHANGES

The impact of student exchanges can be seen through the perspective of the parents, students, and teachers. Parents from a variety of schools and a variety of income levels are the first to say that they can see the exchange experience as "opening the child's mind to different people" and that it "challenges your way of doing things, teaching children that our way in not the only way or the right way." Parents have commented that they see their child return from an exchange with more "emotional growth, self-confidence and maturity, more independence and an appreciation for what they have."

Teachers, who are in schools that facilitate communication from students who go on the exchanges in the form of emails or a blog and also facilitate opportunities for students to talk about their experiences on the exchange, comment that it makes it easy to use maps to show (fourth graders) where our students are visiting. They see older students begin to question the policies and beliefs of Americans. "They see how people from other nations do things and ask why we have a different approach. These types of discussion can arise in just about any subject at the junior high level."

With guided discussion and an appreciation for differences, teachers see the opportunity to "break down stereotypes about the people of other countries." Students who have experienced something with a historical perspective, such as visiting a museum about World War II and the Polish Resistance, can come and talk to younger students who are reading about the Resistance in a class novel. They become a resource about the country that they visited for students across the building.

Among alumni who have participated in exchanges, the appreciation of the experience grows as they become older. A principal of a school with a strong commitment to global education has received numerous emails and comments from alums who visit noting how their elementary experiences with global education have impacted their career path. An alum realized that, "everyone has a different story . . . what they do for fun, what they eat, how they celebrate special occasions . . . it helped me to be open to the 'stories' of the people that I met in high school and college."

PASSPORTS & TICKETS

Passports should be collected by the school office prior to the departure date. Student exchange coordinators have learned from the past experience of students arriving at the airport without their passports (then rushing home to get it arriving back just in time for the flight) that it is safer for school to have all of the passports at least the week before the departure date. At the airport before departure, the chaperones are responsible for checking that all students are present and giving each student his/her boarding pass and passport. Upon arrival at the destination and going through customs, the chaperones need to collect all of the passports and hold them until departure.

In addition to passports a visa is required to enter some countries, for example, Australia and China. To obtain the visa all passports must be sent

Table 3.1 Timeline for Student Exchanges—ISSE Model

Time	Activity	Sample Information
4–5 months prior to exchange	Survey parents interested	Travel to Mexico in the fall, host in the spring, approximate cost $600
4–5 months prior to exchange	Contact Mexico	Twelve students, would like to visit Oct. 4–18, we can host in the spring
4–5 months prior to exchange	Chaperon Selection Formal announcement of Exchange and Parent Meeting for those interested	Mrs. Smith and Mrs. Thompson will be chaperoning the exchange to Mexico. Students will travel Oct. 4–18. We will host April 5–19. Parent meeting for Q&A next week. Deposit due in three weeks.
4–5 months prior to exchange	Students who have committed to going complete ISSE forms for the match of students	Age, gender, interests, family size, pets, allergies
2–3 months prior to exchange	Team USA meetings	Meet every other week for 1–2 hours after school
2–3 months prior to exchange	Reminder to parents	Apply for passport—passport needed earlier for countries requiring visa in addition to passport
2–3 months prior to exchange	Passports sent together to embassy	Apply for visas for countries that require them
1–2 months prior to exchange	Notice to parents	Final payment due
2 weeks prior to travel	Meeting with parents	Information for the trip, e.g. clothes, money, passport, meeting at the airport
Day before or morning of travel	Commissioning assembly at school	Tell the student body about the exchange, introduce traveling students,

to the embassy at least six weeks prior to travel. Schools should consult with a travel agent or the airline for clarification on the need for a visa and the timelines involved.

When working with a school that is not part of an established program, the email exchange should begin with an introduction regarding your school and a statement of goals and objectives in proposing an exchange. This should occur a year or more prior to the exchange. If the school is interested, a Memorandum of Understanding can be created outlining the frequency, length of stay, number of students and chaperones, and any other conditions of the exchanges. The remaining time line can follow approximately the same as that listed in the above table.

DAILY CHECK-INS

Having daily "check-ins" with the traveling delegation is strongly recommended. It ensures that there is a time at the start of each day where the students will see their friends and the chaperones. This check in time should be as close to the start of the school day as possible and needs to be at least 30 minutes long. Chaperones might ask some of the following questions: "How did the evening go?" "Are you sleeping ok?" "Are you eating enough?" "Are there any issues with your host family?" The observant chaperon will be on the lookout for any signs of homesickness.

This is also a time for student and adult members of the delegation to share their experiences. Chaperones also need to go over the schedule for the day and practice classroom presentations or the cultural program. They may also use that time to remind students of ways to interact with their host family or with the dignitaries that they might be meeting that day. The general progression of feelings on the part of the visiting students is:

- First few days—mild to moderate homesickness "Who signed me up for this? What am I doing here?"
- After the third day—students "settle in" and become familiar with their host families, food, and surroundings. They are reassured by seeing their friends each day and they are seeing lots of interesting things.
- Last two days—Students don't want the experience to end. "It went by too fast!" Tears at departing. The more different the culture (language, TV, signs, food, housing), the longer it takes for the students to feel comfortable in the setting.

One student who was a member of a delegation to China commented,

I was a little "shell shocked" at some of the differences. Duck is a traditional food that they eat a lot. I had never had duck before. Parents only have one child and they expect that child to take care of them when they are older. The parents in the family that I stayed with did not speak English so it was like playing Charades to communicate with them. It helped me to be able to email home and to keep a journal. After a few days I realized that this family was like mine. They were really nice and the parents just want you to be happy. The people we met were amazing, even if they didn't understand us. The visit to Liuzhou taught me to be more open to people and that we are different but we are all the same. A smile is universal.

COMMUNICATION WITH PARENTS DURING AN EXCHANGE

Phone calls between parents and students should be discouraged. If they do call, parents, without meaning to, can encourage homesickness by talking about what the family is doing at home. The student focuses on what he/she is missing at home rather than what he/she is experiencing on the exchange. For parents who feel the need to call and talk to their child, it is suggested that they focus on asking their child about his/her experiences rather than talking about what is happening at home.

An effective way to inform parents and school staff about the progress of the exchange is to have the chaperones send a group email each day or as their access to email allows. The group emails summarize the activities for the day(s), students' reactions, observations of how the students are doing, and a note of upcoming events. When possible emails might also include pictures. If there is a specific concern about a student, then the chaperon might email or call the parent.

LIAISON BETWEEN SCHOOL AND STUDENTS

It is suggested that the chaperones meet with the school coordinator of the exchange each day to go over the schedule and to trouble shoot any concerns that host families may have. Other time during the school day can be spent with school faculty in conversations about education, answering questions about education in the United States, observing classes, learning about the scope and sequence of the curriculum, and, if there is an interest, looking at policies and procedures related to the educational program.

HOSTING

Families of students who participate in an exchange need to understand that when the students from the other country come to visit they are responsible for hosting that student. Families can begin connecting with the student that they will host by sending an email welcoming the guest to their home. A letter or email is generally sent from the host student to the guest student and from the host parents to the visiting student's parents. Content of the letters should include but is not limited to:

- Something about their family (parents, siblings, ages, occupations, pets, etc.)
- What their arrangements will be (you'll be sharing a room or you'll have your own room and bathroom).
- The activities that are planned
- Parents assure the visiting child's parents that their child will be cared for as one of their own.
- Letters should close with an offer to answer any questions they may have as they make preparations to travel.

The cost of hosting will vary from school to school. Most schools try to keep the costs to a minimum for the hosting families. Consideration might be given to host families covering the cost of lunch at school each day, transportation, and entry fees for field trips. The recommended guideline is that the visiting student is not to be viewed as a tourist but as one who has come to experience American life. The family should go about their normal routine and include the visiting student as they would their own children. If the family schedule calls for going to soccer practice, visiting grandparents, or going grocery shopping, the student goes along.

Visiting students go to school each day with their host student. Field trips should be arranged through school. If they occur during school time, then hosting parents may go along on field trips, but they do not need to be required to do so.

It is strongly recommended that there is discussion of the types of activities that parents plan to do with the visiting students outside of school time. When some families take their guest to an activity, particularly one that is expensive, and others do not there are frequently hurt feelings among visiting students. Remember these are 10–13 year olds who don't necessarily understand issues of family schedules and finances.

As much as possible there should be some agreement before the delegation arrives about the activities that will be included or not included in the visit. While a consensus is not always possible among parents, the point should be discussed with facilitation by the administration and the coordinator of the exchange.

In some schools, experiences are arranged so that the visiting delegation goes along with a class on their regularly scheduled field trip. For example, the delegation might go to visit the local fire department with a primary class or they may go to the zoo with kindergarten class. This provides students and teachers in the host school time to get to know the visiting delegation and has less overall disruption to the schedule of other classes.

Most schools do not include hosting students on field trips. They follow their regular class schedule and join their visitors only for after-school and evening events. This gives the students a break from each other, minimizes the cost to the hosting families, and puts academics first. The cost of field trips can be held to a minimum with the use of public transportation and walking when visiting major landmarks whenever possible.

Depending on the time of year of the visit, a group outing to a major league, minor league, or favorite town high school or college sporting event might be arranged. Outings that are more expensive such as a day at an amusement park should be discouraged. The overall aim of the program is to keep the cost of hosting to approximately $200.

The general schedule for hosting families involves meeting the visiting student at the airport upon arrival and participating in a few evening gatherings. A gathering at the home of one of the host families or at school on the first evening for a potluck dinner or dessert can be a helpful transition for the visiting students. Just seeing their friends and chaperones a few hours after arriving often helps to keep homesickness at bay.

Additionally, it is suggested that during the course of the two weeks, two or more host families invite the chaperones for dinner so that the chaperones have the opportunity to meet with each of the host families in a more intimate, leisurely manner. Teachers not involved in the exchanges might be invited to these dinners as a way of providing more opportunities for the faculty to interact with the chaperones. On the last night before departure a gathering again at a host family's home or at school for dinner or dessert provides a time for the chaperones and students to say a few words about their experience.

In some schools parents arrange for additional opportunities to gather the visiting delegation and to provide the experience of typical American celebrations. Regardless of the time of year these might include:

- A birthday party
- A pool party
- Halloween
- Thanksgiving dinner

During the day the visiting students should arrive at school in the morning along with their host student. The host school needs to provide a meeting place such as an empty classroom, the cafeteria, or the library for the visiting delegation to meet with their fellow students and chaperones for the daily check-in. The students might be invited to visit every class to give an age-appropriate presentation. The visiting delegation may prefer to attend classes. Art, physical education, and music are the easiest places for visiting students to participate in the lessons. Other classes will depend on the interests of the visiting students.

Class visits for presentations can be scheduled into the social studies time, and the hosting exchange coordinator should do the master schedule. The number of days of field trips is dependent on the budget, school schedule, and overall discretion of the hosting school. Some schools find that two or three days of field trips out of a two-week stay is enough. Others prefer to have more days out of the building.

IMPACT ON STUDENTS WHO HOST A VISITOR

Experiences with hosting a visitor, regardless of whether or not the American student travels abroad, help to broaden a child's worldview. They learn so much by being with a student from another country on a day-to-day basis. Sometimes it's the little things, for example, that faucets are different in another country or that cheese is not easily available in their country. Students see the similarities, enjoying music and shopping. It makes students curious to learn more about their visitor's country. Parents see a greater level of "care" about the people of other countries. "When our visitor's country is mentioned on the news because of the ash from a volcano all of my children wanted to know more about it. They wanted to know if it could have effected our visitor's family and town."

In schools where visiting students go into each classroom to meet with students of every grade, teachers see the benefits for all students. "Hosting students from other countries fosters a culture of openness to learning from others." Students teach the kindergarten students a song from their country or the third graders learn a game from another country. Teachers will see the students singing the song or playing the game at recess. They have a connection to the children from another country. "When students meet children from other nations every year in an environment where parents and teachers value the customs and traditions of others, then they grow up with the knowledge and belief that this is a world where we learn from each other."

When students have met other children from different nations they can see, firsthand, the similarities. "In a setting that fosters friendships they form relationships that override prejudice that might be found in the community or opinions in the media. Meeting someone increases the learning and understanding. It takes away the fear. Take away the fear and you find a friend."

One alum looking back on her student exchange found that it provided "so many teachable moments for my parents . . . helping me understand that our guest had different life experiences." Another student whose family hosted in an exchange noticed that "The kids are so excited to be here. Things that we take for granted are new and different to them so you see your family, your school and the city through new eyes. It makes you kind of appreciate that stuff in a new way."

WELCOME ASSEMBLY

A Welcome Assembly is a wonderful way to celebrate the beginning of a visit from a foreign delegation. Having all of the students in the school gather in one place to "meet" the delegation indicates to the student body the importance of the guests and their visit. It sets a welcoming tone.

In one school the assembly begins with a procession led by two students carrying the flag of the visiting country and the American flag. Host students walk in the procession with their visiting guest student, followed by the chaperones, the principal, and other administrators. The principal opens the event with a history of why the school participates in student exchanges and gives words of welcome to the students and their chaperones. Students stand as both national anthems are played. One by one the hosting students introduce their visiting students and the visiting student says a few words, for example, "I am happy to be here. I hope to learn about your city." This is followed by an introduction of the chaperones and their comments.

The student body can be more active participants in the assembly in a variety of ways. In some schools the students make small paper flags and wave them as the visiting delegations enters and leaves the assembly. In another school a student from each class comes to the microphone for a "pop-up" that is a comment on what their class hopes to learn from the visitors. Some schools have selected students or classes to sing songs of welcome. Music, a universal language, is frequently used to begin and end the assembly. Songs often include the school song, popular songs about friendship, and Beethoven's "Ode to Joy."

It should be noted that if the school is hosting other guests from other countries, such as exchange students, they could also be included in the ceremony. Having the students process in and having their national anthem played is just another way to help students to remember the presence of citizens of other countries.

FAREWELL ASSEMBLY

A farewell assembly with the same basic format as a Welcome Assembly is also suggested. The "pop-ups" from each class would be comments on what the students learned from the visitors. Each student and chaperone might receive a gift of a school sweatshirt, a small stuffed animal with the school name on it or a small stand with the flags of both countries. Comments from the principal or exchange coordinator, visiting chaperones and/or the visiting students complete the event.

FUNDING

Most trips cost between $600 and $1,200 for the students to travel. This includes round trip airfare, passport, a $50 fee if it is an ISSE exchange, a gift for the host family, and splitting the cost of the chaperones' airfare. The cost for each family of hosting should generally be between $200 and $300, which would pay for the student's lunches at school, all field trips and transportation on field trips, and any group activities such as going to a sporting event on the weekend. Families do not need to have a private bedroom for the visiting student.

There are three main ways to fund the exchanges for students. The first would be totally financed by parents. With enough notice, some families can set aside enough money for their child to travel on an exchange. When the exchanges become a well-established part of the school experience, parents often begin saving when the students are in the primary grades so that they have the funds by the time the student reaches junior high.

The second method of financing the trips would be a few fundraising events. The exchange coordinator or the parents of the students going on the exchanges might organize these. Fundraising events can range from selling cookies at lunch to car washes and gift card sales.

The third way to help alleviate the cost of the trips would be seeking sponsors from local merchants or corporations. Some companies that are involved in international trade may be interested in supporting this type of learning experience for students who otherwise would not be able to participate.

EUROCAMP

EuroCamp is 10-day summer camp located in Guentesberger, Germany. Each year students from approximately 16 countries (Austria, Bosnia and Herzegovina, the Czech Republic, Egypt, Germany, Hungry, Israel, Kazakhstan, Latvia, Poland,

Romania, Russia, Senegal, South Africa, Ukraine, Vietnam) gather to engage in typical summer camp activities such as arts and crafts, swimming, and field trips. Students stay in cabins, boys and girls separated, that they might share with students from another nation. Each group has a German camp counselor who is in his/her early 20s to lead them through all of the activities, answer questions, and ensure a positive camp experience.

There is a cultural sharing that is done through a booth-type of display so that students can visit each booth and learn interesting facts about other countries. Chaperones are responsible for getting the students safely to and from the camp location, staying in the cabins at night with the students and for helping with the cultural event. The cost of participating in EuroCamp is the airfare plus a camp fee. For more information about EuroCamp schools should contact eurocamp@kieze.com.

A student that participated in the EuroCamp experience in the summer between seventh and eighth grade and was also a member of a delegation to Mexico for a more traditional exchange compares the experiences:

> On a traditional exchange you learn about one culture, in depth. You see things through their eyes because you are with them 24/7 and you understand that their worldview is different. At Eurocamp there is not the depth of learning about one culture but you are exposed to many cultures, languages and many points of view about the world. You can see the similarities among teens from many countries. We could talk about music and movies. We all pretty much dressed the same. Our group spent a lot of time with the Austrian kids but it was awesome to be part of a concentrated dose of different cultures from around the world!

UNUSUAL OCCURRENCES

An important discussion with parents who decide to have their child participate in a student exchange is the protocol for unusual occurrences. The two occurrences that are considered unusual are a child becoming ill and needing to be hospitalized and a disruption in the transportation home. Suggested guidelines are as follows:

- The chaperones will make the best decision they can given the circumstances—parents will not second guess them.
- The chaperones will communicate as much as they can at the time but may not have access to all of the information that parents want.
- Upon returning home full disclosure will be given.
- In the case of a sick child, parents will be contacted by phone so that options can be discussed.

- Chaperones have a credit card for extraordinary expenses impacting the entire group, for example, travel disruption, and all expenses will be divided evenly by all of the parents of all of the students
- The host school will cover extraordinary expenses incurred in the event of an extended stay and will be reimbursed when the students return to the United States.
- There will be one voice communicating with parents when there is an unusual occurrence and parents need to wait to hear from that chaperone.
- One parent, selected by the parents, will serve as the group spokesperson to the school community or to the press.

INTERNATIONAL PROJECTS WEEK

In addition to traditional exchanges, one school is a member of a six-school collaborative that was formed out of the vision of one principal. The idea of a collaborative group began in the 1960s when a Headmaster of Otto Hahn Gymnasium in Geesthacht, Germany, thought that in order to not repeat the horrors of World War II we needed to help the children from different countries to learn about one another and to develop friendships and understanding. Contact was first made with Dr. Aletta Jacobs College in the Netherlands. In the years that followed Otto Hahn Gymnasium connected with Arpad Gymnasium in Hungary, Lycee Jean Vilar in France, Zespol Szol Chemicznych in Poland, and School #34 in Russia. The German school exchanges student delegations with all its partner schools on a regular basis. Staring in the early 1990s, every three years, delegations from each school attend International Projects Week (IPW) to work collaboratively on a central theme.

After the break up of the Soviet Union in 1990, the transition from a command economy to a market economy resulted in some very difficult times for the people of Ukraine, and many chose to immigrate. A teacher and her family from Kharkiv was one of those. They moved to Germany and were resettled in Geesthacht. When she went to Otto Hahn Gymnasium to enroll her children, she learned of its network of partner schools throughout Europe. In speaking with the Headmaster she mentioned that she knew of an American school that seemed to share a similar philosophy. The connection was made and bi-lateral exchanges between the American school and Otto Hahn Gymnasium commenced. When an invitation was issued to participate in the next International Projects Week in Hungary in 2000, the American school accepted. American students attended IPW in the Netherlands in 2003 and took their turn to host IPW in September 2006.

While this sort of exchange format was specific to this group, the planning and overall format can be used by any school that would like to host two or more schools simultaneously. It also provides another way to have an exchange that is just a week long.

It is best to have a core planning team, made up of the principal, teachers, and parents, to come together to discuss a theme and overall plan for the event. Planning should be done approximately one year in advance of the actual exchange. Funding for such a large multi-national event is certain to be an issue. Financial sources outside of the school's discretionary funds will usually need to be solicited. In one school's case, a graphic designer and a marketing specialist along with a grant writer were brought into the planning group to help with soliciting funds to cover the cost of the event.

It is helpful to have a theme for the week. This sets the stage for the academic events and provides a graphic for publicity. An example of this would be the theme: "The Friendship Project—A Week to Change the World." Using this theme the arts, a universal language, was the focus of the one-week experience. Students were divided into groups, along with the eighth grade students, to work on projects: a quilt made from fabric from each nation, a 60' outdoor mural depicting images from life in each country, a choir, a group that built a 3' peace dove, and a "tech group" that made a video and a newspaper documenting the events of the week.

The marketing group developed a brochure, poster, and stationary that was used to solicit funding to support the event. Within a year approximately $15,000 plus numerous in-kind donations were obtained. Committees were formed to address each part of the week long visit.

A total of 52 students and 16 chaperones from four countries (Hungary, the Netherlands, Germany, and Russia) attended Friendship Project Week 2006. School families hosted each of the 68 visiting delegates for the week. Students from abroad visited every grade sharing their culture and customs with age appropriate information and activities. All of the students participated in a Field Day on teams with students from each grade and students from each nation. On an evening toward the end of the visit, the unveiling of the projects and a cultural performance by each group of visiting students was presented to a "standing room only" audience of faculty, staff, parents, and students. A study conducted by a local university indicated that the experiences were overwhelmingly positive for the host school students, parents, and faculty and for the visiting students and chaperones.

Two surveys were conducted to evaluate International Projects Week. Professors from local universities developed the first. Their goal was to investigate the degree to which the participants in International Projects

Table 3.2 Projects Week Committees

Committee	Task of the Committee
Program/Schedule	Develop a schedule of events for the week
Housing	Match school families willing to host with visiting students and chaperon
Transportation	To/from the airport and all field trips
Pot Luck Picnic	Find a venue (park) and arrange for food & games for 350 people
Hospitality Room	Room in the school for chaperones to go to for meals and "down time," decorations, snacks, drinks, etc.
T-Shirts	Order and distribute t-shirts with logo
Environment	Signs labeling items in all languages in many areas of the building, cafeteria, classrooms, etc.
Welcome Goody Bag	Backpack for each visitor with snacks and gifts that represent the school and the city
Field Day	All day event with students from each nation on teams with our students from each grade, planning games, volunteers, and materials needed
Evening Event for Students & Chaperones	Evening event for students (i.e. sports, mall) and evening out with the teachers
Snack Shack	Low-cost snacks available all day for visitors and host students, volunteers to staff and order snacks
Country Coordinator	Parent volunteer who would be the "go to" person for the chaperones from each country for questions or concerns
Welcome/Farewell Assemblies	Invitation to local dignitaries & lawmakers, decorations, anthems of each country, translations of words of welcome, flags, planning of procession, music and program

Week saw it as "a learning environment that fosters trust, cooperation, understanding and fun." The surveys were distributed to European students, faculty, and administrators and to American students faculty, administrators, and host families.

Responses indicated that the Friendship Project was a positive experience; the Friendship Project was fun, something they would do again if they had the opportunity, and something they would recommend to a friend. The data showed that the experience increased participant's understanding of other countries, promoted better relations between countries, and enhanced trust between people of other countries.

The second survey was developed by the author and was distributed to all school parents, those that hosted and those that did not host, and the faculty and staff. The purpose of this survey was to determine the positive and negative aspects of the experience and to answer the question, "Should we do this again?"; 100% of faculty and staff, 85% of hosting parents, and 47% of parents who did not host a visitor responded to the survey.

The majority of parents, those that hosted and those that did not host, indicated that they thought that their child benefited from IPW and that they would support a future IPW event. All of the faculty and staff indicated that "the time out of class was worth it." There were positive comments from parents: "We should do this again" and "This experience enhanced our commitment to global awareness."

While the faculty and staff have supported the global education program over the years, the reader needs to understand the level of commitment that is present at this time in this school. International Projects Week required the physical education teacher and the art teacher to be totally involved with the projects. Therefore, they were not able to hold classes. Every spare room, the library, gym, and art room were used for working on the projects. One junior high teacher was displaced from his homeroom because that was the classroom located nearest the office and it was used as the hospitality room for the visiting chaperones. All of the eighth graders missed classes for the week as they participated in the project groups. Despite this disruption to the schedule and the loss of class time, the faculty was unanimous in their view that the event was a positive, worthwhile experience and expressed a strong willingness to host another such event. This is truly a reflection of a school culture that values global education.

It was the unanimous decision of the faculty to host another Friendship Project Week in the fall of 2010. The theme for this event was "Hands-On Science." In this instance the students from four different nations were arranged into multinational teams, two students from each visiting nation, along with two American eighth graders. They conducted science experiments with each grade level, kindergarten through seventh grade. With this format the students from each grade worked closely with at least three multinational teams to build something that tested a scientific principal. The act of working together to build something and then testing it gave a common focus and an atmosphere of excitement that allowed students of all ages to enjoy their interaction with the visiting students.

Table 3.3   Friendship Project II

Grade Level	Project
K	What Makes a Rainbow?—After discussing how rainbows form students will create a piece of wearable art using at least four colors of the rainbow.
1	Wiggly, Wiggly Worms—Students will observe worms, conduct simple experiments and explore ways that earthworms help the earth.
2	Feel the Force—Students will engage in a hands-on investigation of magnets.
3	Balloon Car Race—Students will build a light weight balloon powered vehicle and grow in an understanding of the power of air as a force for movement.
4	Egg Drop—After discussion of kinetic energy students will construct and test an egg protection device.
5	Saving Mother Earth—The importance of recycling will be highlighted through the making of recycled paper.
6	Groundwater Sundaes—Ice cream sundaes that demonstrate the effect of groundwater pollution.
7	The Impact of Earthquakes—Using a "shake table" to simulate an earthquake, students will design and construct buildings that will withstand the earthquake.

IMPACT OF SHORT-VISIT EXPERIENCES

The Eurocamp and the Friendship Project experiences differ from traditional exchanges in that they are much shorter in duration, they are more of a whole-group experience, and they are "one-way" visits. Despite these differences they have an amazing impact on the students who participate in them. In these instances the students interact with other students from multiple nations at the same time. They enter a "mini-world" where people from different nations are working for one purpose. It may be sports teams, problem solving, building the most efficient balloon car, field day competitions, or supporting each other as they make presentations and learn about the traditions of their countries.

Because a Friendship Journey format brings 70 or 80 visiting students and chaperones, families across the school are needed as hosts. The increased number of hosting families increases the likelihood that other families, neighbors, and friends of those hosting will have the opportunity to interact with visiting students or adults. Parents comment, "Hosting a visiting student or teacher for one week is easy. It's not a long-term commitment that will take up a lot of your family's time. It's a good way to see if hosting is the right experience for your family." Another parent said, "It's great when so many families are hosting. It becomes a shared experience with friends and neighbors and fun to compare stories with families who host students from a different nation. It's something my kids will never forget."

As the multinational teams interact with each class, teachers see their students with increased interest in looking again at maps to identify the countries represented. "They can see, first hand, that if you are open to it you can work together, play together and learn from each other."

Students in the older grades readily reported observing the overwhelming similarities among teens. They are amazed at how quickly they can become friends with students from several countries despite limited spoken English among some visiting students.

LESSONS LEARNED

- Start with established programs—It is easier to join a program such as the International School to School Experience (ISSE) where the protocols for the exchanges are already in place. Once you have experienced this type of exchange you will have a model for working with other countries.
- Be flexible in all aspects of the exchange—It is important to be flexible as you negotiate the dates of travel. For example, we like to have our students travel over spring break so that they do not miss many days of school. When we propose that time of year we need to be willing to accommodate the time that the visiting school wants to travel. When visiting another country, you need to be very flexible. You don't know the people or the conditions at your destination. So, for example, the mode of transportation, the availability of email, or the room that you have at the school to meet with your delegation each day may not be what you expected.
- Be open to opportunities—You may need to speak to government officials or the school board about your school or the program. You may need to wait after school for your host teacher or be invited to a spontaneous faculty or family gathering. Accept all invitations! While you may be exhausted, these opportunities for short interactions with faculty, staff, extended family, or neighbors of your host teacher can enrich your overall experience.

- Be positive—It is a necessary assumption that everyone is doing the best they can with the resources available. Be a gracious guest that they'll want to have return, not one they'll be glad to see go home.
- What people remember is not so much what they say, but how they were treated.
- Families don't have to redecorate their homes in anticipation of hosting someone from abroad. They've come to meet Americans and see what life in America is all about. Sharing grandmother's birthday is more important than visiting an amusement park.

Chapter 4

Encouraging Teacher Buy In

The benefit of global education when it is part of the culture of a school is that the students begin to initiate the learning among themselves. As I presented a class on water conservation (in a junior high class) and gave an example of shower heads and toilet tanks that we can buy that conserve water at home, one student commented on the toilets in China, another on the toilets in Poland, and a third on toilets in France. This discussion led to the observation that people in other nations walk more and use public transportation that is better for the environment. That led to questions and comparisons about life in America and our use of public transportation and tendency to drive big cars. This came from the students, not from me. They are interested in and able to compare and contrast so many aspects of our lives with the lives of others in other parts of the world. It happens in discussions of weather or natural disasters. They are so aware of other places in the world because of the map studies, student exchanges, and guest speakers that they have encountered over the years. By the time they get to junior high they are applying that information in so many ways.

—Observations of a junior high teacher.

THE INTERVIEW

The key to a successful global education program is the faculty. Without their understanding and support any program is destined to die. For staff new to a school, the place to begin is in the interview. The following questions will draw out a candidate's perspective and initial thoughts on a curriculum that goes beyond one's city, state, and nation.

- Who is your favorite author?
- What kind of books do you read?
- What country would you most like to visit? Why?
- Have you traveled abroad?
- Do you speak a foreign language?
- If a delegation from Country X were to visit our school, how could you incorporate them in your class?
- What advantages or disadvantages do you see in providing students an opportunity to read literature from another culture? What are the challenges inherent in providing that opportunity?
- How would your integrate global education into the subjects that you teach?

While the interview needs to incorporate questions so that the administration has a feel for the candidate's openness to global education, it is also vital that the potential employee understands at that point what they will need to do regarding global education. The following are some of the points that might be discussed or provided in a handout:

- Use of maps in all areas of study
- Integration of international current events whenever possible
- Academic accommodations made for students on exchanges
- Participation in welcome and farewell assemblies (some disruption to the schedule)
- Integration of visiting delegations into class time for class visits
- Integration of information about other countries into basic curriculum
- Flexibility in working with schedule changes when delegations visit
- Collaboration with partner teachers or art, physical education, and music teachers on cross-curricular projects with a global focus

Potential teachers should also know what supports are available, for example, a school's participation in the I*EARN program, software programs, or teachers in the building who use a global focus in the subjects or grade level that they will be teaching.

ENCOURAGING THE USE OF GLOBAL EDUCATION IN THE CLASSROOM

Often members of the faculty who have been employed within the school for a number of years are set in their ways. It may be more of a challenge for them to see the value in changing what they've always done.

When administrators work with faculty members to share ideas, regardless of the subject at hand, it sends two messages. First, this is not a competition. Second, this is a reasonable goal that we all can achieve. The venue for sharing ideas can be small groups such as department meetings or level meetings or a larger group setting such as a staff meeting. Further, brainstorming, discussions, and idea sharing in these settings encourage collaborative ventures across grade levels.

In one school, the junior high department agreed to draw large maps of the continents each month on the playground so that the primary and intermediate grades could "play" on the continents. An intermediate social studies group of teachers decided to put together a cultural fair where groups of students would learn songs and games from other countries. The primary grade students were invited to visit the fair and learn the songs and games.

In schools where students travel to another country, part of the "accountability" upon their return might be that pairs of students visit other classes and present a 10-minute overview of what they learned about the history, government, culture, and traditions. Showing pictures and artifacts will, of course, increase the interest in the presentation. This approach not only shares the learning with other students but also increases the investment of the faculty in the exchange experience.

A rubric is suggested for this type of presentation format so that the students take it seriously and know ahead of time the expectations. The teachers in the classes where they present evaluate the students on their presentation. Some points on the rubric might be the following:

- Organization of information
- Artifacts shown and explained
- Clear explanation of government and history
- Examples of customs and traditions
- Student questions answered

Because one school is strongly mission driven, the agenda at all faculty meetings is organized according to its mission statement. Global education is part of the mission of the school. It is expected at the monthly faculty meeting that there will be information about the global education program: opportunities for students and/or staff, workshops, and community events. Current events in global education become part of the discussion.

Additionally, when a delegation is scheduled to visit, teachers may share ideas about how they plan to integrate the visiting students into a lesson. For teachers who have just returned from chaperoning an exchange, there is time in the agenda to share their experiences as well as their observations of their students, for example, what they learned and what challenges they've overcome. This sharing of ideas and experiences often helps to motivate other teachers in their approach to visiting delegations and to the idea of chaperoning a delegation.

The report from the library includes the list of new titles, videos, or Web sites that include multi-cultural resources, for example, the book of folk tales from Poland or the young adult novel set in Africa. The report may also highlight speakers that are coming to talk to students about different countries. In one school the librarian has the "the Alphabet of Countries" where she has speakers throughout the year for each country of the alphabet. Another librarian has a display that features books that span the grade levels, from a different continent each month.

The report from the art and music departments advise the staff of the new displays going up and the new songs the students are learning that are from other cultures. A report from the physical education teacher would include games or folk dances that students are learning from other countries. The technology teacher offers ideas for projects or Web sites with global topics that teachers can use.

KEEPING WITH STATE STANDARDS

An approach that is most effective in getting the faculty on board is the clear message that, "This is what we do." Teachers may need time and guidance as they look at the state standards for their grade and consider ways to use global education in their instruction. For example,

- When you teach letter writing, have the students write letters to students in other countries through an I*EARN project.
- Use map demarcations to help predict, compare, and contrast weather conditions in other counties for the standard on understanding climate.
- Use information about tall buildings, population size, or the traditions of other countries as your students respond to word problems with the basic math operations.

Once the faculty understands *it's not adding more to their already full agenda, it's doing what you already do differently,* the resistance diminishes.

MAKING THE MOST OF STUDENT EXCHANGES

Not all staff members are in a position to travel abroad with students to visit another school. Nevertheless, they can be part of the experience vicariously through reports from the field. It's possible for the traveling team to send daily reports to each member of the staff via e-mail. Most staff members will be interested in learning about the challenges the students—and chaperones—are facing when they meet the host students, parent, and teachers for the first time in a country where they may not be able to speak the local language or read the newspaper.

The daily reports with photos from the field can be easily uploaded to the school's Web page to create a blog that the entire community can follow. It has been one school's experience that those daily e-mails are then forwarded to grandparents, aunts, uncles, and neighbors. The support for the program grows as additional members of the community share in the experience of the delegation visiting the partner school abroad.

The same holds true when hosting a visiting delegation. A picture is worth a thousand words. That initial meeting at the airport or the look of anticipation in the eyes of the kindergarten students awaiting the arrival of the delegation's visit to their classroom conveys a message difficult to put into words.

With the spotlight on the traveling or visiting delegation, some staff members may feel left behind. A few events can help mitigate that feeling.

- Scheduling visiting delegations to visit each class. This provides each teacher with an opportunity to get to know the students from abroad a bit better. Keeping in mind that *it's not one more thing; it's a resource to be used,* teachers have been known to use the visit to accomplish a curriculum goal.
- If students are expected to conduct interviews as part of the language arts curriculum, the delegation's visit to the classroom is not an interruption, but an opportunity to "check that off the list." Similarly, a public speaking goal can be achieved by assigning students the task of introducing themselves to the visiting delegates. It is one way to provide practice.
- If research skills are part of the curriculum, providing students time to research the culture, customs, and history of the visiting country is a meaningful assignment that can foster engagement through follow-up questions. Not only do students consult standard reference materials, they now have the opportunity to conduct research through interviewing their guests.

- Having a brief social gathering with snacks and drinks for faculty and staff along with the visiting chaperones provides an opportunity for everyone to meet. One school uses a tradition of "toasting" the visiting teachers so that there is a great deal of sharing and laughter. At another school, teachers share one thing they want the visiting teachers to know about their school or community.
- Providing "free lunch" in the teacher's lounge is another way to encourage teachers to go to the teacher's lounge at lunchtime and meet with visiting teachers.
- When hosting parents invite the visiting chaperones to dinner, include some of the teachers so that they have time out of the school day to get to know the chaperones and they get a night out for dinner!

OPPORTUNITIES TO GROW IN AN UNDERSTANDING OF GLOBAL EDUCATION

A good road map ensures that you arrive at your destination without unnecessary detours. A Global Education Program for your school can be your road map. Administrators may want to begin the year with a speaker who has used global education strategies in his/her school. This provides information and allows teachers to have some of their questions and concerns addressed.

The "voice of experience" joining with the administrator can ally fears as a building or district-wide plan is explained. It is suggested that this type of introduction to integrating global education has a teacher-initiated component. Faculty input into a plan increases the level of teacher investment in global education and helps to ensure that the plan is grounded in what are realistic goals for a school.

THE INTERNATIONAL EDUCATION AND RESOURCE NETWORK—PROFESSIONAL DEVELOPMENT

Faculty members are required to participate in professional development each year. When global education is part of the mission of the school or an annual school-wide goal, opportunities in that field are a natural fit. I*EARN, an organization with membership from schools in over 100 countries around the world, is an excellent place to begin. Webinars and an annual conference bring teachers from different countries together to focus on global education initiatives for students from kindergarten through grade 12 in all disciplines: math, science, social studies, language arts, art, music, and physical education.

I*EARN brings together teachers from around the world. Its annual conference is a great place to connect with educators from abroad and build your network of resources. The annual conference rotates among member countries. Because a university hosts the conference with delegates staying in student housing, costs are kept down. With a nominal conference fee, the major expense is transportation to the host site. Conferences have been held in Morocco, Canada, Senegal, South Africa, China, the Netherlands, the United States, Argentina, and more.

Funding for teachers to attend these meetings might be available through professional development funds, grants, or corporate sponsorship. The PTO in one school has committed to funding the airfare for three staff members to attend the I*EARN conference every other year. Teachers attending are expected to share their experience at the conference in the first faculty meeting of the year and to participate in at least one project with schools in other countries in the year following their attendance at a conference.

ACCOUNTABILITY

Global education reaches far beyond student exchanges. It really starts in the classroom in many small ways that are well within a reasonable level of expectation on the part of the administrator. Change, however, is difficult and most of us resist it. Administrators who want to introduce and promote global education in their schools have found a need for some degree of accountability among the faculty.

For some teachers, incorporating global education becomes an annual goal in their professional development plan. This requires documentation of attendance at graduate-level classes or workshops, reading on the topic, or an experience that furthered their growth in global awareness. In other buildings administrators simply observe. They sit in on classes, take note of bulletin boards, and look at lesson plans. Teachers using global education to enhance their curriculum will have evidence of that in any or all of those places.

One school that has a strong global education component to its mission statement bases the annual teacher evaluation in part on how staff members use the mission statement to guide classroom decisions. At a time when there was a possibility of a reduction in force, the staff—not bound by a master contract—asked to be part of the process to redefine the Reduction in Force (RIF) policy.

After much discussion and debate, they recommended, in effect, that those who do not support the mission, all things being equal, be the first to be dismissed if there were to be a reduction in force. The staff firmly believed that the future of the school lay in those who were committed to its mission, not to those who had necessarily been there the longest. They are now required to submit evidence that they actively support the school's initiatives in global education in the curriculum areas for which they are responsible.

- List the titles of books/novels that you and your students read that reflect a variety of cultures and traditions.
- Describe how you integrated the use of maps in all subjects you teach.
- Describe how you have integrated global education into the subjects that you teach.
- List specific ways you supported the student exchange program.
- List professional development opportunities you have taken advantage of to enhance your understanding of other cultures.
- Describe the opportunities you have provided your students to enhance their understanding of other cultures.

This degree of accountability may be appropriate for a setting with a strong commitment to global education and without a collective bargaining group. For the average school setting these questions may be better used as an end-of-year discussion that leads to the planning for the following year. The answers may point to the professional development, the equipment (maps, globes, software, novels), the connections with the community for speakers (ethnic groups, universities, businesses), or the monies needed to support the program.

If this is not what you believe education to be about, if this is not where you want to put your time and energy, then this is not the school for you.

Not all teachers believe in the value of global education. Not all schools are a good fit for some very good teachers. It's about finding the right fit, and this method of accountability enables each staff member to reflect on how good the fit is.

LESSONS LEARNED

- When starting a new program teachers need information and the opportunity to have questions and concerns addressed.
- The more that teachers can initiate ideas that work for their situation, the more likely they are to use them.

- Faculty will follow the lead of the administrators.
- Teachers need to see global education as doing what they already but doing it differently. It should not be "more added to an already full plate."
- Teachers should have resources, such as I*EARN, and the opportunity to network through workshops and conferences available to them so that they do not have to create everything themselves.
- Acknowledge the global education efforts of teachers in faculty meetings, newsletters, etc.
- Making global education part of the job targets or professional development goals helps teachers to keep it on the list of things to do for the year.

Chapter 5

Encouraging Parent Support

You can send e-mails and put notices in the newsletter about global education at your school but that's not what gets parents' attention. It's the children. They are learning about it everyday in the stories they read, the maps they study, the people they meet (speakers, visiting delegations). They come home and they talk about it. They bring home the stories you read together for homework. You get pulled into global awareness because you are involved in your child's education. They are interested in it. They ask questions and even if you've never traveled or met someone from another country you start learning about people from other nations.

—Quote from a parent of children at a school with global education.

INITIAL INTEREST

Some children become involved in sports, music, scouting, theater, or other interests because their parents were, and maybe still are, involved in those pursuits. Other children become involved in those activities because something or someone has sparked their interest. When the parents have no prior knowledge of an activity, they learn along with the child. They go to the practices, the games, the recitals, and the plays. Where they can, they try to help their child learn the skills they need for the activity. Parents become "soccer moms," "boosters for the band," or "theater people."

You may have parents who travel outside the country and are strong believers in having children learn about the people of other nations.

Chances are you will have more parents who have not traveled extensively and feel that learning about the people, culture, and traditions of other nations is not a necessary part of their child's education. Many of these parents will be drawn into global awareness because their children are learning about it.

AWARENESS OF GLOBAL EDUCATION

Creating a school culture that supports global education requires communication with all the stakeholders: students, staff, and parents. Equally as important as support from the staff is the buy-in from parents. Making parents aware of global education in your school is the first step toward gaining parent support.

Some schools find it effective to publicize their global education initiatives on their Web site. It's easily accessible by the larger community and can provide information that most will find interesting and helpful. The school's Web site can be used to communicate the following:

- Curriculum objectives for each grade in areas related to global education (e.g., geography, social studies) can be posted.
- Select a novel set in a foreign country, invite the community to read it as the students do, and conduct a community conversation.
- Rubrics for projects that require students to look at other cultures can be made available to parents and the broader community.
- For those schools with a student exchange program, the students visiting abroad can post daily accounts of their experiences in the host school and country.

Parents looking for a school for their children will consult the school's Web page. It is the preferred method of communication for many, if not most, of the younger parents. The school's Web content can encourage them to find out more about a school or can encourage them to look elsewhere.

Once the prospective parents are in the door, the principal of one school with a strong global education program meets with them to answer questions and to give a guided tour of the building. A walk through the halls covered with projects and artwork that reflects a global perspective is encouraging to those parents looking for a school that will prepare their children to be players in the global economy. Graduation from high school and college are "light years" away from kindergarten, but the foundation for understanding others is laid there. The art they create, the music they make, the books they read, and the poems they memorize are all part of that foundation.

Parents who have made an initial commitment to the school are invited to Kindergarten Round Up or screening in many schools. At Round Up there is another opportunity to share the mission of the school in all areas, reminding the parents why they choose that school for their children. This is another opportunity to highlight global education not only in kindergarten but in other grades as well.

At the beginning of each semester some schools host Curriculum Night or open house—an opportunity for parents to meet with administration and instructional and support staff to learn about the goals in each curriculum area for the four months ahead. It is another opportunity to tell the story of how the students will be challenged, what projects they will work on, what opportunities lie ahead for them to develop their academic and social skills, and of course, the areas of global education that will be covered.

Principals of schools that offer student exchanges use those opportunities to share information that impacts the whole school.

> *In March a delegation of our 7th and 8th grade students will visit our partner school in China and a delegation from our partner school in China will visit us for two weeks in April. Your sons and daughters will have the opportunity to meet them in class and on the playground. Even though your children are in first grade, it's not too early to begin thinking about the opportunities that they will have starting in fifth grade. If you start saving now, you'll have the funding for the airfare when it comes time for you sons and daughters to join a delegation.*

That principal also reminds the parents of the wealth of information that they can find on the school's Web page about all aspects of the curriculum and the many and varied opportunities available to students during and after school. This is also a time to highlight the projects, guest speakers, and experiences that will help to develop the student's global perspective. Pointing out something as simple as a trip to the zoo and how the students will be expected to identify animals from different continents provides parents with a new way of thinking about a field trip to the zoo.

Using the school's newsletter or weekly memos from teachers to parents is another way to communicate to parents what is happening in the area of global education in a particular class, grade, or for all of the students. Some schools feature a grade per week and what they are doing in global education. There is a feature question to go along with the entry such as, "Ask your seventh grader about the Ring of Fire."

ENCOURAGING PARENT PARTICIPATION

The next step in enlisting parent support for global education in a school is participation. It is important to find ways that enable parents to become involved in teaching children about the people of other nations.

Draw on the diversity of your school and your knowledge of the parents. Consider the heritage of the parents at your school. Are they from Vietnam, Mexico, Poland, China, India, or a South American or African nation? Invite parents and grandparents who are natives of other countries to come and speak to some of your students. Many parents are willing to bring artifacts and come in to speak to a class about their native country. This can be a great way to connect with parents and a more interesting lesson for students.

For parents who are hesitant to come in to speak to the class, teachers may want to create a "show and tell" time for students. Individual students can bring in items, music, and pictures from home and present the information to their class. Some students may be embarrassed to present information about their family to their classmates. In this case having the opportunity to present to a class of younger students can be seen as a fun activity and still accomplishes the goal of helping students in your school to be aware of the customs and traditions of the people of other countries.

An additional way to assist parents in sharing their culture but not requiring a school visit is to offer to highlight pictures and other artifacts in a display case in the main hallway. Parents can create a display on their own or with the help of school personnel. Recognition of the parents contributing to the display might be in the display case as well as noted in the school newsletter or on the school Web site.

Enlist parent involvement whenever possible. Using their gifts and talents rather than finances, you bring a wider variety of parents into an awareness of global education. In one school a parent who is a dancer helps students choreograph a dance for the cultural show that students will do when they visit another country. In another school parents come in to help students sew tunics for their International Day program. Cooking traditional foods or desserts for a week of international tastes at lunchtime is way that a third school involves parents.

A parent from China offered a class in the evening for parents and students to learn karate. The list of talents is endless. Teachers and administrators, however, need to take the time to get to know parents who may not speak English. You need to be willing to connect with parents and extend the invitation for participation.

Inviting parents to share their experiences with travel to other countries of friendships with people of other nations is a great way to involve parents directly in the instruction of the students. The more involved parents are in what the students learn the more invested they become in the topic. Global education is certainly part of this equation.

When students in a particular grade are performing poetry, skits, or a short play that has its roots in a different nation, consider inviting parents from a few grade levels rather than just the parents of the students in the performance. It is suggested that a program is provided explaining how this work fits with the curriculum and the school's goal of global education. Similarly, if a visiting delegation is performing a cultural show, it should, whenever possible, be open to all of the students and their families.

If there is a process for families considering a transfer for their children that includes a meeting with an administrator, this is the perfect time to highlight the school's global education efforts. It is another opportunity to share the good news of the emphasis on global education that permeates the curriculum. A page of "Global Education" events might be added to any handouts that are given to new parents. For schools that have traditions in global education or curriculum trends, such as the maps program described in Chapter 2, new parents and students will need to know about this sooner rather than later.

For a global education mission-driven school, the principal takes every opportunity to tell the story of how and when students are impacted and how and when the foundation for openness to the larger world is being built. The principal will emphasize the importance of age-appropriate understanding and appreciation of other cultures throughout the students' elementary and secondary education, because it is those students that will be ready to take advantage of the opportunities presented in college and beyond. They will be a "step or two" ahead of the other students whose vision and experience is more limited.

PARENT INVOLVEMENT IN SCHOOL-WIDE EVENTS

School-wide events such as the Friendship Project mentioned in Chapter 3 or an International Festival can be the best opportunities for involving a large number of parents. These sorts of events require a wide variety of skills and a range of time commitment. The tasks involved are sure to appeal to some parents that would not be inclined to come to school to do a presentation or to host a visiting student.

When considering a school-wide event think first in terms of committees. The basic committees are generally planning, set-up, facilitation during the event, and evaluation. The parents who carry out the direction of each committee may be committing to a very short period of time, for example, a morning or an evening for set-up or a longer time, a whole day or several days, such as facilitation during the event.

Consideration should also be given to support that parents could give to an event from home. This might involve phone calls, sending out invitations, filling gift bags, making signs, or typing up programs. The list of tasks can be endless and tailored to the type of time and support that parents are able to give. The important issue is to offer multiple opportunities for parents to be involved and, therefore, invested in the event and what their child is learning. Too often we assume that parents can't or won't help out. Many times that is due to the narrow choice of opportunities that we offer.

LESSONS LEARNED

- The more that parents are involved as part of a planning committee, being guest speakers, and demonstrating the skills and talents that represent their culture the more they will "buy in" to the program.
- Be sensitive to family limitations in the time and cost involved in projects, student exchanges, and other aspects of global education.
- Clearly articulate to parents the reason for adopting global education as part of your curriculum. As each aspect is introduced, help parents to understand why you are including it in their child's education.
- Be sure that parents know that global education will be a part of your program and it will not detract from meeting state standards or the skill development needed to pass state testing.
- Check in with parents through surveys or an advisory council to see how you can improve global education at your school and/or how parents are receiving your current presentation of global education.

Epilogue

Education in America is at a crossroads. The demands for improved test scores, the necessity of preparing our students to compete with their peers across the globe, and the limits of time and money make this one of the most challenging times in the profession. All are front-burner issues and none will go away. What we have attempted to do is provide a roadmap, a direction, a way forward for those who believe that global education ought to be part of the elementary school experience.

A significant level of global education can be realized without adding anything additional to the already overflowing plates of the instructional and administrative staff. The windows to the world are opened through literature, art, music, and physical education. Examples in math and science can connect those concepts to a global community. With more time but not much more money, another level can be added with the addition of goals in geographic literacy.

For those who can garner the necessary community support, they will discover that a student exchange program connects names and faces with a specific countries and eliminates the stereotypes that prevent understanding and appreciation of different cultures. As part of the journey toward global education, a student exchange program can connect students, their parents and their teachers to people around the world and in the process transform the community.

In 1979–80 an urban parochial school serving an economically and racially diverse population began that journey. Global education became part of its mission. Significantly limited by resources, unlimited by imagination, over 30 years later it continues to offer its students opportunities undreamed of when the idea was first proposed. Every journey takes place because someone wants to go there. They all begin with a single step. If not us, who? If not now, when?

Appendix I

Asia Study Guide
Map Studies Program at Nativity School
Revised July 2004

Students in Grade 4 will be responsible for knowing the location of the following countries and geographic features:

Russia	Tropic of Cancer	Japan	Iraq	India China
Indian Ocean	Pacific Ocean	Himalayan Mountains	Equator	
Arctic Ocean	Arctic Circle	Ural Mountains		

Grades 5–8: Test 1
Students in Grades 5–8 will be responsible for knowing the location of the following countries:

Mongolia	North Korea	South Korea	Taiwan	Papua New Guinea	
Philippines	East Timor	Indonesia	Brunei	Singapore	
Malaysia	Thailand	Vietnam	Cambodia	Laos	
Myanmar	Bangladesh	Bhutan	Nepal	Sri Lanka	China
Maldives	Pakistan	Turkmenistan	Uzbekistan	Tajikistan	India
Kyrgyszstan	Kazakhstan	Hong Kong	Russia	Japan	

Grades 5–8: Test 2
Students in Grades 5–8 will be responsible for knowing the location of the following geographic features:

Sea of Japan	Bering Sea	Yellow Sea	South China Sea	Bay of Bengal
Arabian Sea	Black Sea	Aral Sea	Indian Ocean	Pacific Ocean
Arctic Ocean	Arctic Circle	Equator	Tropic of Cancer	
Indus River	Yangtze River	Mekong River	Huang River	Ganges River
Gobi Desert	Strait of Malacca	Ural Mountains	Arctic Circle	Mount Everest
Mount Fuji	Himalayan Mountains			

Grades 5–8: Test 3
Students in Grades 5–8 will be responsible for knowing the location of the following geographic features:

Iraq	Cyprus	Afghanistan	Iran	Armenia	Azerbaijan	Georgia
Turkey	Syria	Lebanon	Jordan	Saudi Arabia	Yemen	
		Israel				
Oman	Bahrain	Kuwait	United Arab Emirates			

Grades 5–8: Test 4
Students in Grades 5–8 will be responsible for knowing the location of the following geographic features:

Tigris River	Euphrates River	Jordan River	Strait of Hormuz	Sinai Peninsula
Persian Gulf	Red Sea	Mediterranean Sea	Caspian Sea	Dead Sea

Students in Grades 6–8 will be responsible for knowing the capitals of the following countries:

Iran	Syria	Japan	Thailand	Iraq	Turkey
South Korea	New Zealand	Israel	Pakistan	Indonesia	Australia
Jordan	India	Philippines	Lebanon	China	Vietnam
Saudi Arabia	Taiwan	Malaysia			

Appendix II

Nativity School

The Student Exchange Program

1979–80	Mexico	Olinca School	ISSE
	Honduras	Holy Trinity School (h)	ISSE
1981–82	Mexico	John F. Kennedy School	
1982–83	Mexico	John F. Kennedy School	
	India	Bluebells School	ISSE
1983–84	El Salvador	Colegio Internacional (h)	ISSE
1984–85	Mexico	Benjamin Franklin School	ISSE
1985–86	Jamaica	Jessie Rippoll School	ISSE
1986–87	Ecuador	The Jefferson School	ISSE
1987–88	Mexico	John F. Kennedy School	
	Bermuda	Southampton Glebe School	ISSE
1988–89	Mexico	John F. Kennedy School	
1989–90	Mexico	John F. Kennedy School	
	Australia	Belgrave South Primary School	ISSE
	Honduras	Saint John Episcopal School	ISSE
1990–91	Australia	Rowville Primary School	ISSE
	Mexico	John F. Kennedy School	
	India	Bal Bharati School (h)	ISSE
1991–92	Costa Rica	Saint Anthony School	ISSE
	France	Ecole des Brousailles (h)	AFAC
1992–93	New Zealand	Takapuna Normal School	ISSE
	Japan	Katsumi Fujiisi	
1993–94	Ukraine	English Specialist School #3 (h)	CKSCP

1994–95	Ireland	Saint John School (t)	
	France	Ecole Pasteur	AFAC
1995–96	Ukraine	English Specialist School #3	CKSCP
	Finland	Torkinmaki School	
1996–97	Mexico	Nuevo Continente	ISSE
	New Zealand	Takapuna Normal School	
	Kenya	Saint Catherine School	
1997–98	Finland	Torkinmaki School	
	Germany	Otto Hahn Gymnasium	
1998–98	Finland	Torkinmaki School	
1999–2000	Germany	Otto Hahn Gymnasium	
	France	Ecole Crox Boissee	AFAC
2000–01	Hungary	IPW at Arpad Gymnasium	
	Finland	Torkinmaki School	
2001–02	Finland	Torkinmaki School	
	Argentina	St. Peter	ISSE
2002–03	Germany	Otto Hahn Gymnasium	
	Mexico	Princeton School	ISSE
2003–04	Netherlands	IPW at Aletta Jacobs College	
2004–05	Malaysia	Sri Kuala Lumpur Primary	ISSE
	Finland	Torkinmaki School	
	Germany	EuroCamp	
2005–06	Germany	Otto Hahn Gymnasium	
	Malaysia	Sri Kuala Lumpur Primary	ISSE
	Finland	Torkinmaki School	
	Germany	EuroCamp	
	Mexico	Buena Tierra	ISSE
2006–07	Germany	EuroCamp	
	Ukraine	English Specialist School #3	CKSCP
	USA	International Projects Week	
	Finland	Torkinmaki School	
2007–08	Germany	Otto Hahn Gymnasium	
	Finland	Torkinmaki School	
	China	Long Cheng Middle School	
	Germany	EuroCamp	
2008–09	Hungary	Arpad Gymnasium	
	Germany	EuroCamp	
	Australia	Birmingham Primary School	ISSE

2009–10	Poland	International Projects Week	
	China	Long Cheng Middle School	
2010–11	Finland	Torkinmaki School	
	Equador	Jefferson School	ISSE
	Germany	EuroCamp	

ISSE—International School to School Experience
AFAC—Association for French-American Classes;
CKSCP—Cincinnati-Kharkiv Sister Cities Project
EuroCamp—Summer camp in Germany attended by 19 nations

Appendix III

Memorandum of Understanding # 3 2004–07

—Nativity and Torkinmaki

INTRODUCTION

In the global village it is increasingly important for young people to be knowledgeable about and comfortable with people from other countries and cultures. A student exchange program that involves students aged 11 to 13 years provides them an opportunity to expand their understanding of other cultures while still at an impressionable age. Friendships that develop and positive experiences that students have will go a long way to sustaining a peace filled global village. In this Memorandum we outline our vision for the future of the cooperation between Nativity School, Cincinnati, Ohio, USA and Torkinmäki School, Kokkola, Finland.

ACTIVITIES

Student Exchange

Torkinmaki School will invite a delegation from Nativity School to visit Kokkola for two weeks during the summer or autumn of 2004. The delegation will include 2 chaperones and 10 to 15 students. If the visit is in the summer, the Nativity Delegation will have the option of staying at Villa Elba with Finnish students for 5 days. Each family (Finnish and American) will cover the cost of the week at Villa Elba. If the American delegates do not stay at Villa Elba, they will stay with the Finnish families. The decision will be made by the American delegation and the principal of Nativity school by February 1, 2004.

Nativity School will invite a delegation from Torkinmaki School to visit Cincinnati for two weeks during the summer or autumn of 2005. The delegation will include 2 chaperones and 10 to 15 students. The same protocol applies to 2006 and 2007. The Finns will host in 2006 and the Americans will host in 2007. Teachers and students participating will be encouraged to complete the Global Citizenship Project sponsored by the Finnish Association of the United Nations.

Teacher Exchange

During the academic year 2005–06 there will be the option of a 3 week teacher exchange (two or one way depending on finances) between Torkinmaki School and Nativity School. The Teacher Exchange is designed to provide teachers who have not had previous international experience with and opportunity to grow professionally.

The expenses associated with travel to and from the host school are the responsibility of the sending school/visiting teacher. Hosting arrangements are the responsibility of the host school including accommodations, meals and one cultural experience (e.g. symphony, theater, jazz concert). Each participant continues to receive his/her salary from his/her school. The hosting school does not assume any responsibility for payment to the visiting teacher.

Upon the conclusion of the exchange, each participant will write a report on his/her experience outlining what was learned through the experience. The report will be sent to both principals.

Each participant will be expected to complete the Global Citizenship Project sponsored by the Finnish Association of the United Nations.

While visiting the host school, the visiting teacher will be expected to work cooperatively with the host teacher. Duties include, but are not limited to, a presentation to each class in the host school on the visiting teacher's country, school and culture; assisting the host teacher in his/her classroom; and being available to the host community for questions about his/her country. The activities of the visit, the schedule of classes, and the expectations of the hosting teacher will be communicated to the visiting teacher at least three weeks in advance.

Exchange of Student Art

The art teachers will be responsible for an exchange of student art (15 to 20 pieces) once each year, 2003/04, 2004/05, 2005/06, 2006/07. The exchange will occur before October 20 so that the art work may be on display for United Nations Day, October 24.

Bridges of Friendship Between the Families of Torkinmaki and Nativity

The principals will support the development of friendship ties between the families of both schools that may have developed through the student exchange program. They will assist in making contacts and will serve as a resource to the families as they plan the visit.

This Memorandum of Understanding will be referred to the faculty and staff of each participating schools. Modifications to this Memorandum will be possible before it is adopted. The decision to adopt and implement will be made by September 30, 2003.

Agreed to by Mr. Peter Johnson, representing Torkinmaki School, and Mr. Robert C. Herring, representing Nativity School, in the City of Edinburgh, Scotland, UK, on the 15 day of July in the year 2003.

Appendix IV

International School-to-School Experience Forms

Form 7—2006 to be filled out by the participating adult and sent to the host school. Keep copy at school.

**INTERNATIONAL SCHOOL-TO- SCHOOL EXPERIENCE (ISSE)
BACKGROUND INFORMATION ON ADULT**

Name _____ _____ _____ Attach recent
      family name   personal name   initial photo here

Nickname (if any) _____ Male _____ Female _____

Date of Birth _____

Occupation _____

Religious preference (if any) _____

Telephone _____ Email _____

Address _____

Family Members _____

Education: Highest degree _____

      Fields of specialization _____

Favorite activities _____

Likes _____

Dislikes _____

How do you feel you might be used most effectively in the classroom (or in the community) of your host school

_____

_____

What other countries have you visited?

_____

_____

What is your native language? _____

What other languages do you speak? _____

Why are you interested in ISSE? _____

_____

Describe a typical weekend at your home _____

_____

_____

Please make any comments that should be considered in hosting you (for example: smoking or no-smoking environment, meat-eater or vegetarian, allergies, etc.) _____

_____

_____

_____

Rev. 09/06
Form 1—2006 **Application Form** (One to Administrate
Office, One for School.)

INTERNATIONAL SCHOOL-TO-SCHOOL EXPERIENCE (ISSE)
ADMINISTRATIVE OFFICE
586 CLEVELAND AVE.
LOUISVILLE, CO 80027
Phone (303) 666-5010   Fax (303) 494-5908

Name of school _____

Address where all correspondence is to be mailed _____

Telephone/E-Mail _____

The visiting team from the partner school will have no necessary experiences while they are guests in our school community, and the same arrangement will apply while our visiting team is being hosted by the partner school.

1. As a visiting school, we shall try to send a visiting team of boys and girls and up to two adults (including one teacher) of the school (at least 21 years old) to the partner school for 2–4 weeks. Chaperones are not to be a parent from the visiting team.

2. As a host school, we shall locate a home for each of the visiting team from the partner school (students and adults) and will work out a program with them so that each of the children in our school has an opportunity to meet them during the 2–4 week visit.

3. The school exchange fee of one hundred fifty dollars ($150.00 US) is payable for each exchange and shall be sent to the National Representative with the application. However, this fee is not required during the first exchange. Said officer will forward fee to the Administrative Office.

4. Any school not participating in the designated exchange will be charged a $50.00 (US) penalty fee and that school will lose one year of exchange in the next drawing.

    U.S. Schools, only shall forward a $35 registration fee for each member of the visiting team (children and adult) to the ISSE Administrative Office.

_____

The visiting team from the partner school will have no necessary expenses while they are guests in our school community, and the same arrangement will apply while our visiting team is being hosted by the partner school.

Signed _____ Title _____

Print Name _____ Date _____

APPLICATION: The above named school has been accepted into the ISSE program:

National Representative _____ Date _____

Administrator _____ Date _____

PARTNERSHIP: The above named school hereby accepts the invitation to participate in the ISSE program with:

School _____

Hosting Dates _____ Visiting Dates _____

Signed _____ Title _____

Date _____

Form 6—2006   Page 1/ 2 To be filled out by the participating child and sent to the host school. Keep a copy at school.

INTERNATIONAL SCHOOL-TO-SCHOOL EXPERIENCE (ISSE) BACKGROUND INFORMATION ON CHILDREN

Family Name   Personal Name   Initial

_____   _____   _____ Attach recent photograph here

Address _____

Nickname (if any) _____ Male _____ Female _____

Telephone _____

Email _____

Date of Birth _____ Age _____ Grade in School _____

Father's Name _____ Occupation _____

Mother's Name _____ Occupation _____

Other adults living in the home and their relationship

_____

Name of Brothers/Sisters _____

Religious preference (if any) _____

What do you most enjoy doing

  at school? _____

  outside of school _____

Do you take lessons outside of school? _____ If so, what kind? _____

Have you lived in other countries? _____ If so, where? _____

Why do you want to be an ISSE visitor/host?

_____

Have any of your family or relatives been associated with ISSE before?

If so, how? _____

What is your native language? _____

What other languages do you speak? _____

Describe a typical weekend at your home.

_____

_____

_____

Rev. 09/06 1/ 2

Form 6—2006   **Page** 2/2 To be filled out by the participating child and sent to the host school. Keep a copy at school.

Mark only those physical activities, which you enjoy and participate in:

___Tennis ___Swimming ___Gymnastics ___Skating ___Weight Lifting
___Skiing ___Aerobics ___Fishing ___Biking ___Horseback Riding
___Hiking ___Camping ___Gardening ___Jogging ___Water-skiing
___Mountain Climbing ___Rollerblading

Others _____

Group Sports _____

___Football ___Soccer ___Basketball ___Bowling ___Track and Field

Others _____

Dance

___Ballet ___Jazz ___Modern ___Folk ___Line

Mark only those personal habits, which you enjoy and participate in:

___Using makeup   ___Hairstyling   ___Sharing with others
___Being alone   ___Going to Church   ___Playing with animals
___Doing house chores ___Looking after pets ___Trendy and fashionable
___Interest in opposite sex

Others _____

Mark only those creative and artistic activities, which you enjoy and participate in:

___Member of a choir   ___Creative writing   ___Belonging to a musical group
___Cooking   ___Baking   ___Member of a theater group
___Drawing/painting   ___Sculpture/carving   ___Music appreciation
___Playing a musical instrument

Others _____

Mark only those social activities, which you enjoy and participate in:

___Belonging to clubs/organizations (List) _____

___Playing games with friends (specify games
_____

___Talking with friends   ___Playing with older children
___Playing with younger children   ___Talking with adults
___Playing with adults   ___Organizing parties/activities
___Dating   ___Having friends at your house
___Going to friend's houses   ___Talking on the telephone
___Shopping with friendships

Others _____

Please make any specific comments that should be considered in hosting this child (for example allergies to foods, medicines, animals or plants, sleep walking, smoke related problems, health problems etc.

_____
_____
_____

Rev. 09/06

About the Authors

Mary Ann Buchino Ed.D. holds a Masters in School Psychology and a Doctorate in Special Education from the University of Cincinnati. Dr. Buchino has been a school psychologist for 34 years. As a licensed School Psychologist in the State of Ohio for the past 24 years, she has had a private practice serving children with hearing loss and language delays. Working at Nativity School for the past 23 years, she has been intimately involved with and closely monitored the development of the global education program. Dr. Buchino has held an appointment as an adjunct professor at the University of Cincinnati and has presented on a wide variety of topics at the local, state, and national level. Her strong interest in curriculum has led her to research methods for integrating global education as well as consulation on the topic and presentations at the state and regional levels.

Bob Herring earned his Bachelor of Arts and Master of Education degree at Xavier University in Cincinnati. He taught junior high for six years and was principal for five before his appointment as principal of Nativity School in 1984. He is the recipient of the *Global Educator Award* from the National Association of Retired Peace Corps Volunteers (2002), the *Dr. Robert J. Kealey NCEA Distinguished Principal Award* (2006) from the National Catholic Educational Association, and the *National Distinguished Principal Award (2006)* from the National Association of Elementary School Principals and the United States Department of Education.

Index

accountability, of faculty, for global education, 67–68
art, in integration of global education, 7–9

"back to basics" movement, x

chaperones: and costs, 39, 52; daily check-ins, 46–47; email communications with parents, 47; liaison between school and students, 47; responsibilities of, 42, 43, 44, 53; selection of, 40; and unusual occurrences, 53–54
Christmas Card Exchange project, 15–16
Connecting Math to Our Lives project, 16
costs: funding student-exchange travel, 52; of hosting, 48; of student exchange, 38–39
curriculum, and integration of global education: art, 7–9; I*EARN, 15–16; literature, 5–7; maps, 33–34; math, 13–15; music, 9–11; physical education, 11–13; quick tips (lessons learned), 23; science, 18–20; social studies, 16–18; technology, 20–21; world languages, 21–23

daily check-ins, 46–47
A Day in the Life project, 16

EuroCamp, 52–53, 58

farewell assembly, 52
Friendship Project, 54–58
funding. *See* costs

geography. *See maps* entries
Giant Maps Program, 30
global education: accountability of teachers for, 67–68; age for beginning, 2–3; components of, 3–4; coordination of, in schools, 3; currency and pertinence of, 2; defined, 1–2; encouraging use of, in classroom, 62–64; parent awareness of, 72–73; successful, teachers as key to, 61

homesickness, 46, 47, 49
host family, communication with, 42
hosting, 47–51, 89–96

International Education and Resource Network (I*EARN): and professional development, 66–67; projects, 15–16
International Projects Week, 54–58
International School-to-School Experience (ISSE) Program: forms created by, 89–96; and student exchange program, 36; timeline for student exchanges, *45*

language and languages, 21–23
literature, in integration of global education, 5–7

map games, 26–27
maps test: awards for, *32*, 32–33; changes to, by grade, *28*; for grades six through eight, 30–31; introducing, to students, 29–30; number of items on, *29*; special needs students and, accommodations for, 33; student proficiency assessed through, 26–27; World Map Test, 27–29, 31–33
map studies program: and age of students, 26; connecting maps to the curriculum, 33–34; goal of, 26; history of, 27–31; importance of, 25–26; quick tips (lessons learned), 34; study guide example, 79–80
math, in integration of global education, 13–15
Memorandum of Understanding: contents of, 37–38; for student exchange program, 85–87
music, in integration of global education, 9–11
My Heroes project, 15

National Geographic-Roper Public Affairs 2006 Geographic Literacy Study, 25–26
Nativity School, Cincinnati, Ohio: and history of student exchange program, 81–83; role of, in global education movement, ix–xi

parents: awareness of global education, 72–73; communication with, before student exchange, 40–41; communication with, during student exchange, 47; encouraging participation of, 74–75; initial interest in global education program, 71–72; involvement in school-wide events, 75–76; quick tips (lessons learned), 76; as teachers, 22; and unusual occurrences, 53–54
passports, 44–46
physical education, in integration of global education, 11–13
Power Point presentations, 20
professional development, 66–67

school work, missed, during student exchange, 41–42
science, in integration of global education, 18–20
short-visit experiences, 58–59
Sister Cities Program, 36–37
Skype, 21
social studies, in integration of global education, 16–18
spreadsheets, 20
state standards, 64
stereotypes, breaking down, 44, 77
student exchange program: arranging the exchange, 39; benefits of, 35–36; costs, 39, 48; daily check-ins, 46–47; EuroCamp, 52–53, 58; farewell assembly, 52; flexibility needed, 59; forms for, 89–96; Friendship Project, 54–58; funding, 52; history of, at Nativity School, Cincinnati, Ohio, 81–83; homesickness, 46, 47, 49; host family, communication with, 42; hosting, 47–51; impact of, 43–44; International Projects Week, 54–58;

and International School-to-School Experience (ISSE) Program, 36, *45*, 89–96; liaison between school and students, 47; Memorandum of Understanding, example, 85–87; and parents, 40–41, 47, 53–54; passports and tickets, 44–46; quick tips (lessons learned), 59–60; resistance to, 36; and schoolwork, 41–42; short-visit experiences, 58–59; and Sister Cities Program, 36–37; student illness, 53–54; student responsibilities, 41; student selection, 39; and teachers, 65–66; team meetings, 43; Team USA, 42; timeline for, *45*; transportation, disruption of, 53–54; unusual occurrences, 53–54; welcome assembly, 51. *See also* chaperones
student illness, during exchange visit, 53–54

teachers: accountability, 67–68; candidate interview, and perspective on global education, 61–62; encouraging use of global education, 62–64; and International Education and Resource Network (I*EARN), 66–67; as key to successful program, 61; opportunities for, 66; and professional development, 66–67; quick tips (lessons learned), 68–69; and state standards, 64; and student exchanges, 65–66
Team USA, 42
Technology, kinds of, and integration of global education, 20–21, 30
telepresence, 21
tickets, 44–46
transportation, disruption of, during exchange visit, 53–54

unusual occurrences, during student exchange, 53–54

videoconferencing, 21

welcome assembly, 51
world languages, in integration of global education, 21–23
World Map Test, 27–29, 31–33

www.ingramcontent.com/pod-product-compliance
Lightning Source LLC
Chambersburg PA
CBHW082207230426
43672CB00015B/2923